A History
of Political
Scandals

For my wife, Bridget, for caring for me during my illness.

Thank you.

A History
of Political
Scandals

Sex, Sleaze and Spin

Andy K. Hughes

Illustrations by Bea Fox

PEN & SWORD
HISTORY

First published in Great Britain in 2013 by
Pen & Sword History
an imprint of
Pen & Sword Books Ltd
47 Church Street
Barnsley
South Yorkshire
S70 2AS

Copyright © Andy K. Hughes 2013

ISBN 978 1 84468 089 4

A CIP catalogue record for this book is available from the
British Library.

Typeset in Ehrhardt by
Mac Style, Bridlington, East Yorkshire
Printed and bound in the UK by CPI Group (UK) Ltd, Croydon,
CRO 4YY

Pen & Sword Books Ltd incorporates the imprints of Pen & Sword
Aviation, Pen & Sword Maritime, Pen & Sword Military, Wharncliffe
Local History, Pen and Sword Select, Pen & Sword Military Classics,
Leo Cooper, The Praetorian Press, Remember When, Seaforth
Publishing and Frontline Publishing.

For a complete list of Pen & Sword titles please contact
PEN & SWORD BOOKS LIMITED
47 Church Street, Barnsley, South Yorkshire, S70 2AS, England
E-mail: enquiries@pen-and-sword.co.uk
Website: www.pen-and-sword.co.uk

Contents

About the Author

Andy K. Hughes is a successful writer, having already released *The Little Book of Big Words* (2006), *The Pocket Guide to Royal Scandals* (2011) and *The Pocket Guide to Scandals of the Aristocracy* (2012). This is his fourth book, looking at the political scandals from around the world.

Andy spent almost two decades working as a writer, journalist and broadcaster for some of the country's top organisations, including the BBC, ITN and London's LBC Radio and Capital Radio. His writing has also appeared around the world on National Public Radio (NPR) in America and worldwide via BFBS (Forces Radio). Andy has previously reported on the ITV morning news and on Magic Radio.

History has always been Andy's first love and he studied at undergraduate level at the University of Reading before studying for his MA at Oxford Brookes. Research for his PhD is already under way. Andy K. Hughes is now a school History teacher for 11-18-year-olds.

Writing runs in the family; his mother has written a number of books that include *The Pocket Guide to Musicals*, *The Pocket Guide to Classic Books*, *The Pocket Guide to Ballroom Dancing*, *The Pocket Guide to Plays and Playwrights* and *The Pocket Guide to Pantomimes*.

Andy lives in High Wycombe in Buckinghamshire with his wife Bridget, but is originally from Shrewsbury in Shropshire. He has four sons from a previous marriage and five grandchildren.

Acknowledgements

I have been overwhelmed by the generosity of so many people who have given their time and assistance in ways large and small to help me put together this book. First and foremost, my thanks go to my agent (and now friend) Hilary Elston at Straightline Management. Thanks to my wife Bridget, who has again shown incredible patience while I was writing another book and I am indebted to her for her constant support and encouragement.

In addition, I extend my sincere thanks to those who have allowed me to use their photographs, including those who actually went out and took photos for me. They include journalists Nazanine Moshiri, Bill Buckley and Chris Hubbard, as well as friends Verity Bhyre, Aaron Bhyre and Phil Seaman. A big thanks also to gawker.com for their permission to use one of their photographs, and to Jim Fowler in the United States, who has emailed so many people asking for assistance with photographs. Thanks to Hugh Mothersole for his continued support and assistance.

Thanks also for the ongoing IT support from Michael Barry and my son Aaron Mehar-Hughes. Once again, my huge thanks to Nabeelah Ullah, my friend and colleague who has worked tirelessly checking my spelling and grammar. This is the third book she has spent hundreds of man-hours on and I am dreading her calling in the favour! I must thank the staff at Charlton House, the Parliamentary Archives at Westminster and Oxford Brookes University library staff. I need to thank my three sisters, Vicky, Helen and Rachel, for their assistance – from checking my spelling to taking photos, as well as for their general words of encouragement. I am also greatly indebted to my parents and step-parents for their support. Thanks to TCS Autos in High Wycombe for keeping my car on the road during my endless hours of research, even in times of difficulty.

Special thanks to the editor Linne Matthews, illustrator Bea Fox and historical consultant Philip Seaman.

Introduction

A *History of Political Scandals: Sex, Sleaze and Spin* follows on from *The Pocket Guide to Royal Scandals* (2011) and *The Pocket Guide to Scandals of the Aristocracy* (2012). In this new book I have tried to offer a mixture of scandals from history right through to today, from Britain and abroad. I have mentioned the MPs' expenses scandal, but decided to keep it relatively brief; otherwise this massive subject was in danger of taking over the whole book. The first part of the book looks at Britain, the second part the United States and the third part the rest of the world. Stories are in approximate chronological order but because some scandals occurred over a period of time, the chronology can appear slightly out of sync.

As a writer I had been looking forward to putting this book together. We are surrounded by politicians who just cannot help but behave in an inappropriate manner; sometimes I shake my head in disbelief. In addition though, we are also blessed with some fantastic and fascinating political figures. The scandals include passionate affairs (and their offspring), watching pornography at the taxpayer's expense, financial swindling, lies, deceit, arrests, charges, court appearances, bribery, naughty photos (starring in them), naughty videos (starring in them), naughty videos (setting them up) and good old-fashioned punches – both with words and with real fists. When it comes to politicians, there really is no shortage of scandal; some have acted in the most outrageous of ways.

Having analysed the concept of scandal in the previous books in this series, I thought it appropriate to summarise by taking a look at a small sample of dictionary explanations of the word:

- A publicised incident that brings about disgrace (thefreedictionary.com)
- A disgraceful or discreditable action, circumstance etc. (dictionary.com)
- An action or event regarded as morally or legally wrong and causing public outrage (oxforddictionaries.com)
- An action or event that causes a public feeling of shock and moral disapproval (dictionary.cambridge.org)

A History of Political Scandals has touched on all of these. There is certainly public disgrace, plenty of public shock and more than enough outrage at immoral wrongdoings. Of course it comes as no great surprise that politicians, past and present, can provide us with enough scandal to fill a whole book.

It has been difficult to decide which scandals to include and which to leave out. Whilst not wanting to exclude the big ones like Profumo and Watergate, there is so much already written on these scandals that I have kept explanations of them to a minimum. I hope that rather than doing a big story an injustice, a brief account might inspire people who are new to a story to read about it in more depth elsewhere, while readers who have been around a bit longer might enjoy a brief recap.

You will also notice that the majority of scandals in the book are based on male politicians having sex with women they should not be having sex with. These include full-blown affairs or liaisons with prostitutes or, in one case, rumours of spanking underage housemaids. One wonders why relatively few female politicians have gone down this morally bankrupt route. It is true that there are more men at the top in politics, but even taking this disproportion into account, scandal is still mostly down to the men. Perhaps one reason that so many good-looking young women fall for old, fat, balding and ugly politicians is because power is an aphrodisiac. It is probably not quite the same the other way round.

There is one big difference between political scandals and those of royals and aristocrats – and that is 'the voters'. It is interesting to note how public opinion reacts to scandal. How 'the people' felt was not such an important factor with royals or aristocrats in charge. This changed during the nineteenth-century Reform Acts. What is also significant is the reaction and loyalty of a partner. Most people admired Hillary Clinton for standing by her husband Bill when he was accused of infidelity. This, I would argue, was the deciding factor. If she had broken down and fled, the nation might have had more of a 'How could you, Bill – you're wicked' response.

Some politicians can and have survived a crisis. Pamela Druckerman, author of *Lust in Translation: Infidelity from Tokyo to Tennessee*, claims that 'American sex scandals aren't necessarily career killers.' She may well be right insofar as politicians *can* bounce back, and are far more likely to if they have not committed a major crime and were fairly well liked before the scandal broke. Druckerman argues that if an affair is blamed on sex addiction, alcohol or abuse, it is more likely to be accepted and supported by others.

Dishonesty and contradicting oneself are not popular routes to take while a nation is making up its mind. That is why the world was so shocked when Bill Clinton said, 'I *did* have sexual relations with that woman, Miss Lewinsky, that were not appropriate.' This came after he had publicly stated 'I did not have sexual relations with that woman, Miss Lewinsky.' It is not really the sexual act that is the scandal; it is a politician's lying and deceit that causes the real disgrace. There is another point to consider: with aristocrats and royals at the centre of a scandal, one could argue that they had little or no choice about their position in life. However, modern politicians are usually regular people who have chosen to live and work in the limelight and yet some do not understand that that means leading a wholesome, perfect life.

Chapter One

United Kingdom

John Wilkes MP – bribery and libel

English politician John Wilkes (b.1725 d.1797) led an eventful life, both privately and professionally. He was the son of a successful malt distiller and was educated at an academy in Hertford, and then privately tutored. In 1747, he married Mary Meade, who was heiress of the Manor of Aylesbury. This union brought him a comfortable fortune and respectable status among the gentry of the county of Buckinghamshire. Wilkes was profligate by nature and was a member of the Hellfire Club, which indulged in debauchery. Wilkes bribed voters so he could win an election to sit in the House of Commons in 1757.

His time in Parliament was rather chequered, including him unwisely attacking the government in his journal *The North Briton* in 1763. He was continually prosecuted for libel, expelled and re-elected. He was the original comeback kid and survived all the scandal. He was generally regarded as a victim of persecution and a champion of liberty. Wilkes was a very popular man and enjoyed much support.

After winning a seat in the 1768 election, Wilkes was arrested and taken to King's Bench Prison for writing libellous material against the king and government. A large crowd of supporters gathered at St George's Field, near the prison. Around 15,000 people arrived outside the prison and chanted in support of Wilkes and against the king and the government. The authorities were worried that the crowd would try to rescue Wilkes, so the troops opened fire and killed seven people. There was widespread anger at the Massacre of St George's Field, as it came to be known, and this led to a number of disturbances all over London.

George Canning MP – from Downing Street to pistols at dawn

Canning (b.1770 d.1827) only served 119 days as British prime minister, one of the shortest on record. However, rewind two decades and Canning was at war with a fellow cabinet minister, Viscount Castlereagh. The man known for his opposition to parliamentary reform and for his big speeches outside Parliament resigned from his earlier post as Foreign Secretary in the Duke of Portland's government over his scandalously acrimonious working relationship with the War Minister, Castlereagh. The pair did not see eye to eye, especially over certain military matters. In fact, the two men had become arch-enemies.

In September 1809, Castlereagh discovered that Canning had plotted to have him removed from the Cabinet. Tempers flared and eventually Castlereagh challenged Canning to a duel. On 21 September 1809, they fought their duel, both battling for their honour. It was a complete disaster involving two respectable gentlemen. Canning had never fired a pistol in his life and completely missed. Castlereagh shot Canning in the leg. The childish and scandalous behaviour resulted in both men resigning their government posts.

Canning lost out to Spencer Perceval in his bid to become prime minister. This may have been twisted good luck, as Perceval became the first PM to be assassinated during his time in office. A man called John Bellingham shot Perceval in the lobby of the House of Commons on 11 May 1812, having

Today, a statue of George Canning overlooks the House of Commons. (Kieran Hughes)

Canning's Berkshire residence during his political heyday. (Kieran Hughes)

a personal grievance relating to compensation for his time in jail abroad. Canning later replaced Castlereagh as Foreign Secretary in Lord Liverpool's government after his old rival killed himself in 1822. Canning went on to replace Liverpool as PM on 10 April 1827. A few months later on 8 August 1827, he died from pneumonia.

Canning has since come to be seen by many as a 'lost leader', with a lot of speculation about what he might have achieved if he had lived.

Assassination of Prime Minister Spencer Perceval

At the time of writing this book, only one British prime minister has been assassinated – Spencer Perceval (b.1762 d.1812), although the IRA has come close to increasing that number on two occasions; once in 1984 during the Conservative Party conference in Brighton, and again in 1991 when it fired missiles that landed in the garden of No. 10 Downing Street. The Brighton bombing is discussed in later pages. Obviously it is scandalous enough that a prime minister is assassinated at all but I also want to address some additional scandals surrounding the Perceval assassination.

John Bellingham was a Liverpool trader of mixed success who had traded with and visited Russia as part of his work. There was a business dispute in Russia and he was imprisoned over an alleged debt. He sought help from the British ambassador in St Petersburg, as well as from other officials. Little help was given and it was more than five years before Bellingham was freed and he returned home. Once home with his wife and family he started to seek compensation from the British Government for his time served in jail. He did not get very far and was brushed aside, despite his determined and polite efforts. Even his wife told him to give up his crusade. Bellingham was rather bitter so he travelled to London, where he visited the House of Commons to make sure he knew who the leading politicians were. He then had a special pocket sewn into his jacket to conceal a gun, planning to attack the very heart of the government. Bellingham was not part of a religious or political group; he was a lone man upset with the hand dealt to him by the government. So after one official told him to 'do his worst', that is exactly what he did. At 5.15 pm on 11 May, as the Tory prime minister, the Rt Hon. Spencer Perceval entered the Commons' lobby on his way to a debate over trade restrictions, John Bellingham shot him at close range in front of a lobby full of people. He was immediately apprehended. The prime minister said, 'I am murdered', and fell face-down on the floor. Just minutes later, a local surgeon declared him dead as he examined him in a nearby room.

John Bellingham assassinates Prime Minister Spencer Perceval in the House of Commons entrance lobby. (Illustration by Bea Fox)

Bellingham was arrested, locked up, tried and hanged within a week. At his trial he blamed the government for not freeing him from his imprisonment and compensating him. He apologised to Mrs Perceval and her children. Previously he had said that he had shot the politician, not the man. The scandal of a prime minister being assassinated was followed by a scandal of improper justice. The government had panicked; it had been a knee-jerk reaction. To understand the situation one must be able to put events into historical perspective and see them through the eyes of the people in 1812 rather than in the eyes of people today. There had been huge political and industrial unrest in the country and many feared, without any evidence, that the assassination was a signal for riot or revolution. Was the rush for justice the reason why there had not been enough time to certify whether or not Bellingham was insane or why he was not given enough time to organise a proper defence? Despite the nature of his crime it was certainly a scandal that the court demanded that Bellingham enter a plea before any consideration was given to his defence team being allowed more time to prepare a case. In fact, papers needed for his defence had been taken off him. In addition, his legal team had only had a few days' notice to prepare for the hearing. And as John Bellingham himself pointed out, he was in the unusual position that his prosecutors were also the witnesses against him. His legal team wanted to make a case for his insanity but they would have needed more time to investigate. The Attorney General made flippant remarks in court as to why Bellingham was not insane. Mollie Gillen, in *Assassination of the Prime Minister: The Shocking Death of Spencer Perceval*, said that regardless of innocence or guilt, Bellingham's trial was a complete travesty, and to quote Lord Brougham, at the time, it was 'the greatest disgrace to English justice'. The jury took only fourteen minutes to decide the guilt of John Bellingham. The whole hearing and verdict had been rushed.

According to the Old Bailey records, the recorder, Mr Shelton, said to the prisoner, John Bellingham, that he stood convicted of the wilful murder of Spencer Perceval and asked him why the court should not give him the ultimate punishment of death, which it could do so according to the law. When Bellingham refused to comment the sentence was pronounced. The recorder told Bellingham: 'Prisoner at the bar, you have been convicted by an attentive and merciful jury.' He went on to describe the crime (the assassination) as malicious and atrocious. To a silent courtroom he then announced that he would pass the most dreadful sentence (i.e. the death sentence). He told Bellingham: 'You shall be hanged by the neck until you be dead; your body to be dissected and anatomised.'

If indeed John Bellingham was insane – and historians still debate this issue – the case may have been handled differently. However, the big rush to get a conviction to avoid civil unrest was carried out at the cost of giving a fair trial. It reminded me of the US government's attitude to a fair trial after the capture of the former Iraqi leader Saddam Hussein, almost two centuries later, when it told the media: 'We'll give him a fair trial and then we'll hang him.' Then again, the US kept many prisoners in Guantanamo Bay without any trial at all – a scandal in itself. Well, it was a scandal that Bellingham was not allowed the luxury of a fair trial; it was both a political and a legal scandal.

Bellingham was hanged near Newgate Prison in London. When his body dropped through the hole and he was dangling by the neck, several men went below the scaffolding and tugged hard at his legs. This is what they did to

St Luke's Church, Charlton, where Spencer Perceval is buried. (Kieran Hughes)

men (and women) who had been hanged. Some were still alive and by pulling hard it made sure the job was finished. It was seen as a merciful thing to do. After John Bellingham was hanged a hush fell over the crowd. He had many supporters, people who hated the government, and Perceval, in particular. Spencer Perceval was buried at St Luke's Church in Charlton, his coffin taken through the big wooden doors to its final resting place. All this was just a few yards from his former family home, Charlton House.

New literature on the assassination, *Why Spencer Perceval Had to Die: The Assassination of a British Prime Minister*, by Andro Linklater, takes a deeper look at the likelihood of a further scandal in that Bellingham had

The heavy wooden doors through which his coffin was carried on his last journey. (Kieran Hughes)

St Luke's Church. (Kieran Hughes)

St Luke's Church tower. (Kieran Hughes)

Charlton House, the former Perceval family house and estate, now open to the public. (Kieran Hughes)

not worked alone. Linklater claims that there is a possibility that Bellingham was financed by others. Perceval certainly had his enemies; he was anti-slave trade, which Liverpool depended heavily on for its economic success. In fact, there were scenes of jubilation and celebration in some parts of the country following his assassination. In a bizarre case of history almost repeating itself, when former Prime Minister Margaret Thatcher died in April 2013, there were scenes of celebration by some who claimed to hate her; again, many of these were in Liverpool. The background and reasons for Perceval's death have been covered in a number of books, including those by Mollie Gillen and David C. Hanrahan. Both historians closely examine a number of questions over the assassination, including suspicions, reactions and ramifications.

Nineteenth-century dissection and resurrectionists

The death sentence has always been the ultimate sentence for all sorts of civilisations, but occasionally it has been given an extra twist. In Tudor times, for example, you might have been *almost* hanged to death but then made to watch your insides being ripped out and burnt on a fire in front of you, before you took your last breath. In the case of John Bellingham, his body was handed over for medical dissection. It was meant to add to the terror of the death penalty. This particular part of the punishment continued in England and Wales until 1832, when the Anatomy Act was passed. The Act required anatomy schools to be licensed and make detailed reports to the Home Office of where each body had come from.

Once again, it is natural for us to see events of the past through modern-day eyes. We take it for granted that our doctors, surgeons and nurses know how our bodies work. But this is only the case because in the past inquisitive medical men dissected bodies to learn about how they function. In the late-sixteenth century, for example, one could study anatomy at Padua or Leiden. At Leiden, the Anatomical Theatre was established in the 1590s and it was where public dissections took place in front of large audiences. Artists like Rembrandt and Hogarth captured the dissections in their images. This led the way for the regular dissection of the executed.

The practice became common on the Continent and in Britain. According to Barry and Lesley Carruthers, in *A History of Britain's Hospitals*, the Royal College of Surgeons was allowed to purchase the bodies of the hanged from Tyburn, and they were sliced open from top to bottom. The account tells of at least one case when the person was still alive when they were put on the dissecting table after having been hanged.

The demand was enormous and people who became known as resurrectionists would steal bodies from graves. A black market developed and bodies were even imported. Events got so nasty that relatives would stand guard over the graves until the body of their loved one had rotted beyond use. Alternatively, gravestones in churchyards were often surrounded by heavy iron bars to stop the grave robbers getting hold of the body. They were called mortsafes.

Dissection was where criminality met respectable medicine. A number of well-respected surgeons were accused of collaborating with the grave robbers. When the practice was banned in Scotland, medical students simply moved south. The 1832 Anatomy Act resulted in dissection becoming more controlled. It was at this point that hanged criminals such as Bellingham were no longer taken to be dissected. Only the bodies of the deceased from workhouses and hospitals, if not claimed by relatives, could be sent to the

Examples of the heavy-duty graves used to keep out the resurrectionists. (Helen Benson)

anatomy schools. As a result of the Act, grave-robbing died out. In 1812, Bellingham would have known that the ultimate punishment was death and dissection, but he thought that once he could show his grievance was fair, people would understand. Even in his letters from his cell in Newgate Prison to his wife back home, he intimated that everything would turn out just fine and he would soon be home. This, however, is further evidence that he was insane and it was a scandal that his lawyers were not given time to prove it.

Sex, lies and Lord Melbourne

Lord Melbourne (b.1779 d.1848) was prime minister twice – from July 1834 to November 1834 and then again from April 1835 to August 1841. He was a Whig and known to be young Queen Victoria's favourite. He tutored her in world politics and the workings of government. For many years people have debated the 'closeness' of these two important figures. It was unlikely to be sexual as the young queen saw him as a father figure, and even gave him use of a private apartment in Windsor Castle.

Melbourne, who was born William Lamb and succeeded his elder brother as heir to his father's title in 1805, was a scandal magnate. His wife, Lady Caroline Lamb, had a very public affair with the poet Lord Byron. In 1812, this was Britain's biggest political scandal; everyone was talking about it! Melbourne was humiliated by his wife's actions. He parted from her and

Windsor Castle, where Lord Melbourne enjoyed his own apartment, courtesy of the young Queen Victoria. (Kieran Hughes)

there was a formal separation in 1825. Lady Caroline died three years later, at the age of forty-two; Melbourne was dutifully by her side. She had spent her life drinking, taking drugs and having an affair. King William IV appointed Melbourne prime minister in 1834.

Melbourne was accused of sleeping with a married woman, Caroline Norton, and was taken to court by her husband. This affair threatened to bring down the government. Caroline Norton's husband accused Melbourne of taking part in spanking sessions with his wife. Then came the shocking accusation that Melbourne regularly spanked young aristocratic ladies as well as orphaned young girls; the latter were kept at Melbourne's house and disciplined by the whip. The spanking and stripping of the young orphan girls caused quite a stir at the time and tarnished Melbourne's reputation. It was a scandal that almost brought down the government.

Prime Minister William Gladstone and the prostitutes

In the uptight Victorian times you would have thought that senior politicians might have been careful about their behaviour. This was not the case, as William Gladstone (b.1809 d.1898) proved. He is considered as one of the great British parliamentarians of our time, but his interest in prostitutes always had him dicing with scandal.

Gladstone's lifelong love of prostitutes started when he was at school at Eton in the 1820s. Even after his marriage in 1839, he continued to spend his money on ladies of the night. By the time he was Vice President of the Board of Trade in 1843 (then President) in Robert Peel's government, he had managed to curb his addiction. However, this was short-lived and he was at it again within a few years, even inviting girls back to Downing Street when he became prime minister. By 1851, he was visiting a prostitute called Elizabeth Collins every few days. His 'habit' continued through his chancellorship from 1852, and he became the victim of attempted blackmail after someone saw him with a hooker. As prime minister, he carried on seeing prostitutes, and later in life he was still at it – even at the age of eighty-two. He had often gone about his business by pretending to visit girls to try to save them and read to them from the Bible. His competitor Benjamin Disraeli once joked about Gladstone going out to 'save' girls and asked him to save one for him!

The website of the British Government concentrates on Gladstone's 'rescue and rehabilitation' of prostitutes, claiming he was merely walking the streets 'trying to convince prostitutes to change their ways.' gov.uk/ government claims that Gladstone spent a large amount of his own money on this type of work.

Bad boy Disraeli

Benjamin Disraeli's (b.1804 d.1881) political service to his country spanned more than three decades and included two terms as prime minister; the first time for nine months in 1868, and the second time for a lot longer, from February 1874 to April 1880. London-born Disraeli started to study law but abandoned his studies, preferring classic literature. He had some success as a published writer – something that he liked to joke about with Queen Victoria, as she too had had some work published. He was well travelled throughout Europe, an experience that resulted in a bad case of venereal disease. He was known for dressing in black, loving velvet clothes, for being rather dandy in his appearance and for being a brilliant debater. He was England's first and only Jewish prime minister and is perhaps best remembered for bringing India and the Suez Canal under control of the Crown.

Disraeli's feud with Gladstone was very public, and the Queen is said to have hated Gladstone too. Disraeli's desire to get into politics saw him stand unsuccessfully in Wycombe in June 1832, and several times again in the same town as well as in the Taunton by-election in April 1835, in which he was also unsuccessful. After his failed attempts to get into Parliament, in 1837 he was elected as Peelite for Maidstone. (The Peelites were a mid-nineteenth-century breakaway faction of the Conservative Party, initially led by Sir Robert Peel and later joining forces with Radicals and Whigs to create Liberals.) He was ridiculed during his acceptance speech but said, 'The time will come when you will hear me' … and he was right. He also won the seat for Shrewsbury in 1841.

It was Disraeli's business dealings and love life that created some of the scandal around him, but he survived them all. If he had been in office today I doubt whether he would have survived politically. His scandalous life was not without consequence though. It was his failed business dealings that put him on a slippery, scandalous slope. He borrowed heavily to invest in South American

Prime Minister Disraeli, commonly referred to as 'Dizzy'. (Illustration by Bea Fox)

mines. In the early 1820s, still a young man, he ploughed substantial amounts of money (other people's money) into these foreign investments, hoping to make his fortune. But all did not go well. In December 1825 there was a huge crash in the City and Disraeli lost everything. His shares were not worth the paper they were written on. He was twenty-one and owed thousands of pounds. He spent years avoiding his backers and running up further debts. It was an embarrassing occasion when, just as he was trying to get elected in Shrewsbury in the 1841 election, his opponents plastered details of all his debts on posters around town. Disraeli carried on and held his head high. His debts at the time exceeded £20,000. However, his writing, with several published books, had given him some income.

In 1827/8, in between his failed business ventures, his writing and eventual political career, Disraeli suffered a nervous breakdown. In the 1830s, Disraeli was known for his affairs with a string of women, mostly much older than he. However, it was one particular relationship that caused a huge scandal in its day – his relationship with the married Henrietta Sykes, daughter of a wealthy brewer. Henrietta, mother of four, wife of eleven years of Sir Francis Sykes, was regularly seen on the social circuit with Disraeli. Sir Francis allowed the liaison to continue as he was busy sleeping with one of Disraeli's former lovers. The strange disjointed foursome lasted until 1836. A year later when he entered Parliament, scandal followed him, when a lawyer from Maidstone accused him of bribing voters and then not paying up. Disraeli libelled him in a newspaper and the lawyer successfully sued him. Matthew Parris and Kevin Maguire call Disraeli 'a genius' in *Great Parliamentary Scandals*, referring to his ability to take the heat off himself by creating a different problem.

In 1852, Disraeli became Chancellor of the Exchequer in Lord Derby's minority government, and when Derby retired in 1868, Disraeli became the new prime minister. On finally achieving his ambition, he said, 'I have climbed to the top of the greasy pole.' In 1874, the Conservatives achieved a huge election victory and Disraeli became prime minister again. By now he was seventy years old. He was, however, greatly affected by the death of his wife in 1872. In 1879, Disraeli was elevated to the House of Lords as the Earl of Beaconsfield and Viscount Hughenden. He died in 1881 aged seventy-six. On his deathbed he apparently said, 'I had rather live but I am not afraid to die.' He was buried at Hughenden Parish Church in Buckinghamshire.

Some of the major Acts of Parliament that went through on Disraeli's watch included the Conspiracy and Protection of Property Act 1875, which decriminalised work of trade unions and also allowed peaceful picketing. In addition, the Public Health Act 1875 was passed, which improved sanitation and living conditions in dirty towns.

The 1890s' Liberator Building Society scandal

The Liberal Party MP Jabez Balfour was first a working man's hero for encouraging grafting men to save hard and buy their own home. Jabez Spencer Balfour was born in 1843. He later liked to be referred to as J. Spencer Balfour. He became Liberal MP for Tamworth and later Burnley, Mayor of Croydon and the name behind the Liberator Building Society. However, his business empire, including the building society, was not all it seemed and disaster loomed.

This was Victorian Britain, where thousands of families worked long, hard hours and were slaves to their weekly rent collections. The Liberator's aim was to give hope to hard-working families so they could save to buy their own home, giving them security. The Liberator became one of the country's biggest financial institutions on the back of a massive property boom. Balfour displayed his wealth by having a big house and lots of fine possessions and clothing. His appearance was that of a very wealthy man. He invested in a flat in London and an estate in Oxfordshire. He made a few enemies along the way by pulling down old run-down cottages and replacing them with rows of modern houses.

As the final decade of the nineteenth century appeared, it was clear that all was not well, despite Balfour venturing into banking and construction. There was a downturn in the economy, and when that happens, people always look harder at those looking after their investments and money. Investigations showed that Balfour's success was largely based on optimism and hot air, with the company's turnover exaggerated on paper to allow big pay-outs for Balfour and his associates. The company and its associate companies were revealed as shallow failures; they collapsed. Balfour had been cooking the books, and borrowing from Peter to pay Paul.

It was not just the Liberator and others in the group that collapsed; with them collapsed all the little savers and investors. Thousands of people were left penniless overnight. There was no massive government bailout. It was not unusual to hear of people taking their own lives when they found out all their savings had gone. Balfour did not stick around to face the music, or the wrath of his customers. He disappeared to South America straight away and managed to stay on the run for three years. He was eventually dragged back to Britain, where he served twelve years in prison.

After his release from prison in 1906, Balfour stood firm over his pride for the buildings he had been instrumental in making. He invited everyone to judge him for his buildings, suburban estates, London mansion blocks and, his *pièce de résistance*, Whitehall Court, which was the pioneer of the fashionable flat system in London. Whitehall Court is a massive block that was built between 1884 and 1887 between Whitehall and the Thames Embankment. Balfour's blocks of flats were ultra-modern, with lifts, electricity, ornate doorways and other mod cons. Famous residents of Whitehall Court have included George Bernard Shaw, H.G. Wells and Lord Kitchener. Flat No. 54 was headquarters for MI6 during the First World War.

Balfour's life ended in scandal and many of his investors lost everything. But perhaps he was right to tell people to judge him on what he had built. He has left us with many buildings that will survive many more years to come.

The Marquess and the Marconi shares

The first Marquess of Reading (b.1860 d.1935) failed to make his fortune on the London Stock Exchange when he was plain and simple Rufus Daniel Isaacs. He was about to run away overseas in 1884 when his mother persuaded him to stay and study to become a lawyer. It turned out that this was his natural gift. By 1898, he had been made a Queen's Counsel and became a well-known name after working on some high-profile cases. With a number of honours awarded to him, he turned to politics and was elected to Parliament in 1904 as a Liberal Imperialist. He was made Solicitor General in 1910, and then Attorney General. Despite a knighthood and his new position, he did not make it to his desired position of Lord Chancellor. This was because of his involvement in the Marconi scandal.

This British political scandal broke in the summer of 1912 under Asquith's Liberal government. It was all about high-placed government figures profiting from insider trading and privileged business knowledge. The government of the day was on the verge of issuing a contract to the English Marconi Company that would be very lucrative. Several government officials privy to this knowledge bought shares in its sister company in the United States. Names at the centre of the insider trading scandal included Lloyd George, who was Chancellor of the Exchequer at the time, Sir Rufus Isaacs, Postmaster General Herbert Samuel, and the Treasurer of the Liberal Party, the Master of Elibank, Lord Murray. Corruption centred around Rufus being in the Cabinet and his brother being a director of Marconi. The corruption and scandal left a nasty taste in the public's mouth as many were angry at the sneaky dealings of politicians to line their own pockets.

It was not until 1913 that Isaacs became Lord Chief Justice. He lived at Foxhill House in Earley, Berkshire, and was elevated to the Peerage as Baron Reading of Erleigh in 1914. He was created Viscount Reading two years later, and Earl of Reading, along with the subsidiary title of Viscount Erleigh, in 1917. In addition, he was made Viceroy of India in 1921, and then Marquess of Reading in 1926. He was knighted in 1910.

Foxhill House in Earley, former home of the Marquess of Reading. (Kieran Hughes, taken with kind permission of the University of Reading)

Horatio Bottomley MP – journalist and great swindler

Horatio Bottomley (b.1860 d.1933) was a British financier, a journalist and an MP, as well as a newspaper proprietor. He was quite clever at getting people to part with their money to invest in his many and various schemes. He was orphaned at a young age and started his first job at fourteen as an errand boy for a London firm of solicitors. He witnessed first-hand one of the clerks adding a fictitious tax to clients' bills, and then duly putting the extra money in his pocket. He eventually found his way into journalism, and then several years later, in 1888, founded the *Financial Times* newspaper. Bottomley was the newspaper's first chairman. He claimed to be a man of the people and his journalism exposed several scandals. He entered Parliament in 1906 as the Liberal MP for Hackney South, and was re-elected in 1910. In 1912 he went bankrupt and lost his seat.

However, Bottomley was a corrupt, champagne-loving, womanising rogue who tried to make a fast buck wherever possible. He first promoted a company called the Anglo-Austrian Union. This was supposed to buy companies in Austria, and he managed to raise £93,000 with which to operate. Bottomley took just over £88,000 of that for himself. The company obviously did not succeed, but Horatio went on to try again, setting up a company called the Hansard Union. This time, he raised £1 million. Its biggest investor, holding a 25 per cent stake, sent in an investigator and found that £600,000 of the money was totally unaccounted for. Bottomley now faced charges of fraud and was brought before the courts. The judge seemed to like him and dislike the prosecutors, steering the jury into a not guilty verdict.

Bottomley got up, dusted himself down and started again. This time he began to promote the shares of an Australian gold-mining company. He managed to sell around 10 million shares with forged certificates. There was another investigation; Horatio was charged with fraud and managed to get off yet again.

Bottomley had made quite a bit of money at the expense of others, and liked to drink and gamble it away. However, he did use it to set up a weekly magazine called *John Bull*, giving itself a patriotic voice during the First World War and calling Germans 'Germ-Huns'. Of course, he charged for competition entries and made a large sum of money. He charged a lot for his speaking rallies, acting as an unofficial recruiting agent for the war effort. It's thought he made about £27,000 from these rallies. He managed to get himself re-elected to Parliament on an independent ticket in 1918, on a big majority. He promised he would look after the interests of those who had served their country in the war.

In 1919, he launched another one of his dubious money-making schemes. It was just after the end of First World War and people had been urged by the government to buy Victory Bonds. It was a way of bolstering the economy. However, at £5 each, they were too expensive for many people. Horatio's *John Bull* started the Victory Bond Club. Readers could pay as little as £1, which would go towards buying bonds, and prize draws would share out the interest earned on them. Many ex-servicemen were among the contributors. Cash and cheques poured into *John Bull's* London office, adding up to hundreds of thousands of pounds. It all started to go wrong when some early subscribers wanted their money back, claiming that they had not received their Bond Club tickets. This gave the scheme a bad name, and others wanted their money back too.

In the autumn of 1919, one of Bottomley's associates, Reuben Bigland, was desperate for some cash. He had helped Bottomley out of a few problems in the past and so asked him for help. Bottomley refused and this was the beginning of the end for him. Bigland was so angry that he promised revenge. He sent out thousands of leaflets describing Bottomley's scheme as his 'latest and greatest swindle'.

Bottomley took Bigland to court for libel and blackmail, claiming he had demanded money, but Bigland was acquitted on both charges. Then, in May 1922, Horatio Bottomley MP appeared at the Old Bailey charged with fraud. The truth about the Victory Bond Club and his other schemes was told in detail. It turned out that huge sums of money had been taken from them to pay his debts. From the Victory Bond Club alone, £100,000 had been taken. Bottomley was found guilty and was sentenced to seven years' penal servitude, losing his political position and his reputation. He was released five years later and tried to embark on a speaking tour and launch a new journal. Both of these ventures failed because of his ruined reputation. His wife died in 1930, his daughter emigrated and all but one of his friends deserted the pathetic figure and broken man, no longer the once-flamboyant political hero and businessman. Only his friend Peggy Primrose stood by him and took him in. Horatio Bottomley died of a stroke at Middlesex Hospital in May 1933.

Downfall of the nineteenth-century railway king, George Hudson

Hudson (b.1800 d.1871) was a hugely influential and successful man, as Lord Mayor of York, as MP for Sunderland, as a businessman, as Deputy Lieutenant for Durham and as a magistrate in York, as well as several other places. He climbed to the top of the ladder and spectacularly fell all the way down to the bottom. It was the middle of the nineteenth century and the country was gripped by railway mania. Everybody wanted to invest in the railways, climb on board or get work in them. They were rather like today's internet, being the communication spectacle of their day.

Hudson was one of the biggest investors during this time. He became a very powerful man. Hudson was born in 1800, 12 miles outside York, in a place called Howsham. He was the son of a farmer and ended up as the man York had to thank for its major role in the country's railway network. The former draper's apprentice inherited £30,000 from a great-uncle, although some say under rather suspicious circumstances. Later, Hudson joined the Tory Party and by 1835 was elected to York City Council. A few years later, he became the city's Lord Mayor. He used his dubious inheritance to invest in the new railways.

In 1833, he bought 500 shares in the construction of the York to Leeds and Selby railway line. As the largest shareholder he used his influence to get the London to Newcastle line to go through York, which was not the original plan. Hudson became chairman of the York & North Midland Railway Company during an era of rail mania. George Stephenson was the company's engineer. Within a decade, Hudson was known as the railway king, with 1,000 miles of track under his control. He became very wealthy and invested in land in Yorkshire. Meanwhile, his companies controlled more than a quarter of England's network and he was investing millions of pounds in projects.

George Hudson was one of 155 MPs who had directorships of railway companies. This opens the doors for accusations of unfair dealing at best; corruption at worst. But it was all rather normal in those days. However, Hudson's dealings were rather more scandalous. He actually bribed his colleagues so bills would get through the House that allowed him to complete more railway purchases. He might have got away with it in the middle of the nineteenth century, but today that would be a huge scandal. In *George Hudson: The Rise and Fall of the Railway King (A Study in Victorian Entrepreneurship)*, A.J. Arnold and S. McCartney described Hudson as 'not technically gifted … proved to be a very able promoter and organiser who became king of the railway world by the early 1840s … soon acknowledged as the best railway manager in the country.'

By 1848, Hudson's success was running out of steam. His business practices were coming under scrutiny. In *Great Parliamentary Scandals*, Parris and Maguire claimed that keen-eyed shareholders began to study the accounts because they had become suspicious and found a number of discrepancies. The shareholders were right; Hudson's payment of dividends out of capital was revealed and this had a severe knock-on effect on his companies' share prices. A number of investigative committees were set up to examine Hudson's investments and his buying and selling of shares (and the timing of them, to be more precise). Hudson's position had become untenable and he had to resign. The dividend payments had become a national scandal and he was also forced to resign from a number of his company directorships. Large sums of money classed as 'misappropriated' had to be reimbursed. Even his political career was affected and he had to resign from the city council. His brother-in-law was also accused and the strain was too much for him; he killed himself. George Hudson's questionable business dealings were splashed across many newspapers and he was seen as a disgrace. He was determined to hang on to his parliamentary seat, and he did so for a few more years, even winning in the 1852 election. In 1859, however, he lost his Sunderland seat.

Compared to some of the great financial swindlers in history and some of the great business conmen and political scandalmongers, Hudson was not all bad. He juggled the finances and cooked the books, bought and sold shares with insider knowledge and used his position to further his corporate power. He was imprisoned for just over a year at York Castle because of money he owed to shareholders. Friends had managed to join forces to raise the money owed and Hudson was released in 1866. George Hudson died almost penniless in 1871.

Labour's first sleaze

There is a saying that most Labour scandals are about money and most Conservative scandals are about sex. One could argue either way on this theory, but one important Labour MP proved that it was indeed all about the money.

John Belcher was parliamentary secretary to the Board of Trade in Attlee's 1948 post-Second World War government. Belcher had become associated with a lobbyist called Sidney Stanley and it was not a terribly healthy working relationship. Stanley was very good at showering gifts on Belcher, including tickets to sporting events, clothes and holidays. Stanley, in the meantime, was going around boasting that he could get Belcher to put in a word about an investigation into a company that had breached rationing rules. An inquiry was set up to investigate the claims and Belcher resigned his position and stood down as an MP in February 1949. His resignation is seen as Labour's first real sleaze scandal.

Tom Driberg MP – a close shave with scandal, more than once

The sexual antics of Tom Driberg (b.1905 d.1976), MP for Maldon in Essex and later Barking, never really made the headlines in a major way. He was corrupt and well-connected. These two 'qualities', along with a lot of cheek and good luck, managed to keep his shenanigans out of the newspapers. On a more serious note, he had a lot of friends in MI5 and MI6, as well as in the national press. He was also a KGB spy, codenamed Lepage.

Driberg was accused of being an Eastern Bloc agent by two Czechoslovakian defectors to Britain. In 1928 he joined the *Daily Express* as a gossip columnist. His parliamentary success started by winning seats in 1942 and 1945, first as an independent and later as a Labour Party candidate. Driberg left the House of Commons in 1974. There was always a serious feat that he would expose any parliamentary male colleagues he had shared affections with if he was ever outed and shamed as a gay man. He was an overtly promiscuous and predatory homosexual in the days when it was not acceptable. He once claimed that sex was only enjoyable if it was a one-off, with someone whom you did not know and would never see again. His predatory behaviour was well known in Westminster and his homosexuality was the worst kept secret ever! He believed that there was no such thing as a heterosexual man; in other words, he could persuade any man to welcome his affections. It is well known that he had many sexual encounters.

Driberg's unfinished autobiography was quite sexually graphic and told the stories of his many encounters, from school to university, and finally as a politician, describing his conquests and what he did with them. He talked about his love of toilets and cottaging. He was known for his dirty mouth and outrageous, often offensive, use of sexual overtones.

Driberg had his fair share of close shaves with scandal, including a trial for indecent assault on an unemployed coal miner after touching his groin. In fact, he was repeatedly caught by the police in homosexual acts committed in the street or public toilet, and by his own admission bribed his way out of it. Party conferences were a particularly busy time for him, when he would pick up as many as he could. He had two close shaves during his time as an MP, including a sting by a policeman posing as a gay man; an agent provocateur.

Driberg hated men with beards; it was his sexual idiosyncrasy. There was actually an increase in Labour's bearded men during his time at Westminster. His promiscuity perhaps had a serious effect on his career as, despite his talents and knowledge, he never rose through the ranks of his party.

There was great surprise when, in 1951, Driberg announced his intention to marry a woman called Ena Binfield. Thinking her rather plain, Winston Churchill looked at her photo and claimed, 'Buggers can't be choosers.' Many felt sorry for Ena and others could not understand what Driberg was playing at. Perhaps it was a plan to make him look more respectable and further his career. In 1975 he was created Baron Bradwell. A year later, he died from a heart attack in the back of a taxi in London, rushing to a lunch appointment. No doubt, he took some of his naughtier and more scandalous secrets to the grave!

The Coldstream Guard turned MP – found in a bush

Another decade, another MP, and yet another gay scandal. This time, Oxford-educated Ian Harvey, with his enviable CV – including his presidency of the Oxford Union, war service and impressive parliamentary career – messed up in 1958. The Parliamentary Under-Secretary of State at the Foreign Office was found in the bushes at St James's Park with a member of the Coldstream Guards. Harvey tried to escape but was eventually caught by police and subsequently arrested. Perhaps not his best decision, he tried to give a false identity to the police but was caught out. The shame was all a bit too much for Harvey and his political party. He decided to give up both his job and his parliamentary seat. This was not the last we ever heard of Ian Harvey though, who made a comeback with two titles; Vice-Chair of the Campaign for Homosexual Equality and also as Chairman of the Conservative Group for Homosexual Equality.

The Profumo affair

This is usually voted the number one political scandal whenever there is a poll or survey about political scandals. So much has been written about it over the years, including autobiographies and personal accounts, films, articles and songs. It has become a part of our nation's political history. Even the great scandals like Watergate and Clinton/Lewinsky do not quite match the credentials of the Profumo affair.

Let us first take a look at the characters involved:

- Harold Macmillan: Conservative Prime Minister at the time
- John (usually called Jack) Profumo: Secretary of State for War in Harold Macmillan's government
- Stephen Ward: Well-connected society osteopath and so-called pimp
- Christine Keeler: Pretty 19-year-old showgirl who slept with Profumo
- Mandy Rice-Davies: Keeler's friend
- Yevgeny Ivanov: Russian naval officer and suspected spy
- Lord Astor: His party at Cliveden House brought them all together

Lord Astor had a gathering of friends at his grand home, Cliveden, in Berkshire, in 1961. Keeler spent time living with Ward and he introduced her to a number of well-known people. At this party she met the Secretary of State for War, John Profumo. He first spotted her climbing naked out of a swimming pool as he was walking by with his wife. It was obvious immediately that he fancied her and, despite his wife being present, he later made a pass at the beautiful Miss Keeler. It was the start of an affair that was to bring down a government.

This was more than a straightforward love affair. There was a suspected complex triangle of deceit. MI5 was concerned about Keeler's relationship with the Russian naval officer Yevgeny Ivanov. The intelligence agency was concerned that he was manipulating her to try to get sensitive information from Profumo to send back to Moscow. It was a politically sensitive time, during the Cold War, when the Russians were treated with suspicion.

It was only when one of Keeler's previous partners appeared on her doorstep and shot at it that things became public. The police had been called, the press began to sniff around and before long the whole relationship was out in the open. However, in 1963, with the affair now public knowledge, Profumo was trying to save his job and issued a statement in the House of Commons insisting that he did not have sexual relations with Keeler. He was, of course, lying to the House and could not get away from it forever. He made another statement, on 5 June 1963, admitting that he had lied to the House and then stepped down as an MP.

Perhaps that could have been the end to the whole story, but it was not. Stephen Ward was arrested for living off the earnings of prostitution. Ward took a fatal overdose; one conspiracy theory claims he was murdered by MI5, although there is no evidence to support that. Harold Macmillan's government never recovered from the scandal. It was one of the reasons it lost the General Election the following year. Macmillan himself fell ill later that year and resigned. Keeler was given a nine-month stretch in Holloway for perjury.

The scandal heralded an era of more openness, more investigation and more questioning. Society's leaders were no longer trusted as they were before. Nothing was done discreetly again and fewer blind eyes were turned. The Profumo affair, more than any other, showed the weakness and vulnerability of the human beings at the very top of society.

Profumo died in 2006, after years of working in the charity sector, raising awareness and money for the most vulnerable in London's East End. He had become a well-loved man who had more than served his sentence and repaid his debt. He and his wife Valerie stayed together and remained friends with the late Queen Mother and the Thatchers. Valerie died in 1998.

One of the most recognisable images of Christine Keeler is the photograph of her sitting astride a chair, seemingly naked, although with nothing on show.

It was taken in 1963 by a photographer called Lewis Morley in a room upstairs at Peter Cook's Establishment club in Soho, London. Today, in its brochure, Cliveden House, where Profumo and Keeler met, describes how fortunes have been made there, plots hatched and the course of history changed.

The scandal of John Vassall and secrets sent to the Kremlin

When we think of scandal and the Macmillan government we normally think about the Profumo affair, but the seeds of bringing down the government were planted many months before. In September 1962, Prime Minister Harold Macmillan was unhappy that an arrest had been made at the Admiralty. The scandal affected a Cabinet minister, a junior minister and an unknown clerk called John Vassall (b.1924 d.1996). It was a big scandal and Fleet Street journalists made a meal of it. Vassall was jailed, there was a certain amount of shame and jobs were lost! Even two journalists were jailed. And this is why Fleet Street was angered. After all the scandal and fuss, we can see why Macmillan was sorry that a spy had publicly been caught. Macmillan's view was that a spy should never be caught. He should be identified and controlled.

In historical context, it was a really bad time for a spy to be discovered. It was the middle of the Cold War, days before the Cuban Missile Crisis, and just after the Portland spy ring had been discovered. The press went to town on the government's lack of security. Vassall had been photographed by Russian intelligence while dancing naked at a gay party, wearing his underpants on his head and a big grin on his face. The blackmail started with Vassall passing secrets to the Russians and ended with a high-profile trial at the Old Bailey in 1962, and an eighteen-year jail sentence. The police who had raided his London apartment in 1962 found photographs of more than a hundred secret naval documents that concerned the authorities as potentially damaging in the wrong hands. Vassall admitted that he had been supplying the Soviets with similar documents for six years.

Vassall had been assistant private secretary to the Civil Lord of the Admiralty and had access to top-secret documents. The press were demanding to know how Vassall had gone undetected for so long and reported on the risk to the country's security. They wrote a lot of nasty things about the spy: his mixing with perverts, his liking of wearing women's underwear and quotes from old school pals who called him a sissy and poked fun at his homosexuality. Former government colleagues distanced themselves from the scandal and the press asked all sorts of questions about Vassall's dubious finances, and how nobody noticed the large amount of money he had. He was living beyond his means, residing at a luxury flat in Dolphin Square, Pimlico, London. Even certain politicians were demanding to know more about Vassall's finances and why his activities had gone undetected.

The press started to scrape the bottom of the barrel and interviewed Vassall's cleaner to see if there was a sexual link between Vassall and his boss, Thomas Galbraith, Lord of the Admiralty. The discovery of private letters between Galbraith and Vassall created more scandal and Galbraith resigned from the government. There was no evidence of impropriety but questions were being asked about Vassall's and Galbraith's loyalty to the nation. Some suspected they were going to leave the UK and defect.

Meanwhile, Prime Minister Harold Macmillan had heavily criticised the press for its handling of the whole affair. He accused the press of conducting itself terribly, without any sense of responsibility. A tribunal established that there had been no impropriety in Vassall's relationship with Galbraith, who, although he felt obliged to resign his post, later received a more senior government job. Meanwhile, two journalists were sent to prison for refusing to reveal their sources. Some suspected that the tribunal had been set up to attack the press. The relationship between Macmillan and the press had turned sour and the prime minister would pay for that dearly in the approaching Profumo affair.

Vassall did not spend the entire eighteen years behind bars; he was released after ten years' detention, mostly at Maidstone Prison in Kent. He was a free man in 1972. He had never really been a committed communist or communist sympathiser, unlike men such as Burgess, Maclean, Philby and Blunt. He had been motivated by greed though, and because the Russians had threatened to post pictures of Vassall taking part in the gay orgies to his mother. After doing his time, Vassall went on to do a number of low-key administrative jobs, as well as releasing his autobiography. He died in 1996.

Enoch Powell and the 'Rivers of Blood' speech

Shadow Defence Secretary Enoch Powell (b.1912 d.1998) was a British politician, classical scholar, writer and soldier. He made what he called his 'Birmingham speech', and what others called his 'Rivers of Blood' speech, on 20 April 1968, at the Midland Hotel in Birmingham (now called the Burlington, on New Street). At the time the Labour government was getting ready for the second reading of the Race Relations Bill. Enoch Powell's carefully timed speech, from the opposition, was an attack on this anti-discrimination Bill. Powell saw it as a pathway to immigration without any restrictions. He knew exactly what he was doing and how controversial his speech was going to be. He had told journalists that his speech would go off like a rocket.

The speech prophesied about non-white people who would use health and education resources at the expense of white people. He painted an image of the white man being a stranger in his own country. He quoted from Virgil's Greek epic *The Aeneid* about the river Tiber foaming with much blood. Thus, his racist speech was dubbed the 'Rivers of Blood' speech. Conservative leader Edward Heath fired Powell from his shadow cabinet immediately. There followed protest marches and strike, letters of support, and messages for and against Powell's message. He claimed he was relating the fears of one of his constituents. This man had apparently told Powell that in this country in fifteen or twenty years' time, the black man would have the whip hand over the white man. The man expressed a wish that he and his family should move

Burlington Hotel, New Street, Birmingham. This was formerly known as the Midland Hotel, where Enoch Powell MP made his famous 'Rivers of Blood' speech, 20 April 1968. (Bill Buckley and Rommel Siangco Catalan-Buckley)

overseas. Powell meanwhile warned of changing neighbourhoods and plans and prospects for the future defeated. In his speech he tells the story of an old white woman who sees her street taken over by 'negroes', a word he used several times, and how they had harassed her.

All this was thirteen years after the black American woman Rosa Parks refused a bus driver's instruction for her to give up her seat for a white man. Enoch Powell was still calling a black man a 'negro'. Enoch Powell's clear racism was scandalous enough by today's standards. But what made his extreme views even more dangerous was his ability to mesmerise an audience with his expert oratory skills. Norman Shrapnel's and Mike Phillips's article 'Enoch Powell: An enigma of awkward passions', in *The Guardian* in February 2001, said that whether Powell was truly a racialist was a matter of semantics. They pointed out the irony of his bravest and most passionate speech where he had demanded the exposure of British maltreatment of Mau Mau suspects in Kenya ten years earlier. Other than that, Enoch Powell had spoken little on immigration, certainly in his early career. In the interest of historical balance, Enoch Powell's academic, military and other political work for his country should not go unrecognised. He had served as a Conservative Party MP (1950-1974), Ulster Unionist Party MP (1974-1987), and as Minister of Health (1960-1963).

John Stonehouse MP, the politician who faked his own death

In true Reggie Perrin style, an MP and government minister left behind his clothes on a beach in Miami in November 1974 to fake his own drowning. But this was not Reggie Perrin; this was John Stonehouse (b.1925 d.1988). In the 1970s, the fictional TV character Perrin left his clothes on a beach to fake his own death. The real-life John Stonehouse did the same.

Stonehouse had held a number of important positions in Harold Wilson's government, including that of Postmaster General. It is thought that during this time he met his future secretary, mistress and eventual wife, Sheila Buckley. His affair was Westminster's worst-kept secret, although his wife Barbara did not know about it for a very long time. When Labour lost the election in 1970, Stonehouse failed to get a Shadow Cabinet position, and focused his life on trying to be a successful businessman. It seems as though he was not as clever in business as he was in politics and the strain of the web of his twenty companies proved too much for him in the end. To avoid the writs and investigations he looked for an easy way out, and so faked his own death. The House of Commons even held a minute's silence for him and began to prepare a by-election to replace him. Even his wife and children were convinced he had died. There was no reason for anyone to suspect foul play at this stage. It was rather surprising for everyone when he re-emerged safe and well in Melbourne, Australia, with a new identity and his secretary Sheila Buckley by his side. Australian police arrested him on Christmas Eve 1974. At first they were unsure of his real identity and suspected they had the missing aristocrat Lord Lucan, who was wanted for questioning in relation to a murder case in England and who had been missing for a while.

Following his extradition to Britain, Stonehouse stood trial in 1976 and was sentenced to seven years for fraud and deception. In August 1979, the former MP for Walsall was released from prison, refusing to speak to anyone before being driven away at high speed. His health had been in a poor state behind bars and he had suffered three heart attacks. He was released on bail after serving three years of his seven-year sentence.

Just when you thought you had heard enough scandal about one person, there is even more! Stonehouse was also accused of being a spy for the Czechs. However, there was never any proof he handed over sensitive information. In 1980, the then prime minister, Margaret Thatcher, decided to keep all this quiet on the basis that there simply was not enough evidence. John Stonehouse and Sheila Buckley got married in 1981 and they had a child together. They lived a relatively quiet life, but sometimes appeared on chat shows. Stonehouse died in 1988, at the age of sixty-two.

The Jeremy Thorpe scandal

This can be classed as one of the world's most famous political scandals – in the same class as Watergate, Clinton/Lewinsky and Profumo. It has been written about widely over the years and so a brief mention and acknowledgement will suffice here. Of course, its main content, homosexuality per se, is no longer a scandal in this context.

Oxford graduate Jeremy Thorpe was a successful politician, becoming leader of the Liberal Party in 1967 at the very young age of thirty-eight. In 1969, a man called Norman Scott claimed that he and Thorpe had been lovers a few years previously. This was at a time when homosexuality was still illegal in the UK. The scandal got worse years later, when allegations emerged that a hitman had been hired to kill Norman Scott.

In court in 1979, Jeremy Thorpe was cleared of any involvement and completely exonerated. The judge attacked three star witnesses for the prosecution and called Scott a liar. Thorpe's lawyer was George Carman, no less, who demolished the prosecution witnesses. In a calculated and clever move he also stopped Thorpe from taking the stand. When the *Daily Express* looked back at the scandal in 2009, it said, 'No political scandal in modern British history has ever come close to matching the explosive affair of Jeremy Thorpe.' After the trial, Thorpe retired from public life and in 1999 published his memoirs, *In My Own Time*.

Harold Wilson offers hard cash to Colonel Gaddafi

When Gaddafi was in charge of Libya, he was funding the IRA and its attack on the British mainland. Secret files, recently released, show that in the 1970s, Prime Minister Harold Wilson and the Labour government offered to pay Libya £14 million to stop supplying the IRA. It was hoped that the longer-term effect might encourage trade between Libya and Britain. The offer was made personally from Wilson to Gaddafi.

Government minutes from 1977 show an eighteen-month negotiation between Her Majesty's Government and the Libyan authorities. The overall aim was to settle a dispute over a cancelled contract for tanks and missile systems that Libya had ordered from Britain, various trade matters and the arms-to-IRA issue. There is no evidence that the UK actually went ahead and paid any money to Libya as a result of the negotiations.

James Dunn and the shoplifting spree

James Dunn (b.1926 d.1985) was elected Labour MP for Liverpool Kirkdale in 1964, taking on the roles of government whip and later Junior Minister (Northern Ireland). However, on 27 July 1979, he went to the Army & Navy Store in Victoria, Central London, and helped himself to a few items. Having seen him stuff a number of items into a bag, two store detectives followed Dunn as he left through the front entrance. They caught up with him in a nearby stationer's shop and he said he wanted to tell them everything in private. The police were then called to deal with the situation. Dunn had two ties, a sweatshirt and a couple of armbands secreted on his person. The total value of the haul was a little over £15.

The case went to the Inner London Crown Court in May the following year. Dunn said that he associated one of the store detectives with a man he had to deal with in Northern Ireland and that he panicked. Dunn's defence was based around his state of mind at the time. He admitted taking the goods from the store, but he pleaded not guilty to the court. He blamed exhaustion for his behaviour, which the judge had called 'out of character'. He had been taking anti-depressants and sleeping pills and said that he could not even remember what had happened on the day he took the goods from the Army & Navy Store.

Despite Dunn's poor state of health, which the judge had recognised, the 54-year-old MP was found guilty by the jury and he was conditionally discharged for a year, with £100 costs. Dunn defected to the SDP in 1981, but his career took a slide soon afterwards. He lost his seat in the 1983 General Election. He died in 1985.

The selling off of Britain's council houses

As with all political decisions there are two sides to every argument (or more, perhaps). However, some would say that the Thatcher government's decision to promote the Right to Buy Scheme in the 1980s decimated the country's social housing stock. Since the scheme, even after Thatcher, almost 2 million people have bought their own council house. So where is the scandal? The most dim-witted social scientist should have been able to forecast that future generations of people in need of social housing would be chasing an ever-decreasing national stock of council houses. The scheme was based on the

Council houses sold into the private sector. (Kieran Hughes)

assumption that it was better to have a property-owning nation, making it more prosperous. Critics have been quick to ask where future needy families would live. At the time, Thatcher was accused of bribing voters. The government of the day said the policy was a good way of redistributing wealth throughout the nation, helping people who otherwise would not be able to afford to get onto the property ladder.

The scheme offered discounts of up to 50 per cent if tenants wanted to purchase their housing. There was a cap of £25,000, and this was increased to £50,000 by 1989. The big sale was part of Thatcher's decade of privatisation, which saw British Telecom, British Steel and many other national firms being sold off to the country's citizens. Since 1980, nearly 2 million council homes have been sold in England, but only about 350,000 have been built to replace them. That is a significant shortfall. Additionally, regional differences have rarely been taken into account. For example, if a council house is sold in Putney and one is built in Rhyl, this would cause significant geographical problems. The Blair government reduced discounts massively and almost stopped the scheme, but it was revived by the Cameron-Clegg coalition in 2012. Housing charities argue that the few homes that have been built to replace the stock are rented at 80 per cent of the market value, instead of 40 per cent in the pre-Right to Buy days. That means fewer people get social housing and when they do it is at greater expense. Critics of the scheme argue that this is a social and political scandal that will affect future generations of Britain's lowest socio-economic groups.

Depending on which newspapers you read, there has always been a variety of reactions to the news that more council houses will go up for sale with big discounts, guarantees for mortgages and other helpful measures. Some say replacing them with new builds would create jobs and put money into the economy. Critics will point out that some recipients of the big discounts could one day pocket the difference through their own private sale or rental deal. What *is* a scandal are the millions of homeless people in Britain at any one time. Whatever the plus sides of encouraging home ownership and the economic betterment of a few in the short term, the scandalous lack of looking to the future and asking where the children and grandchildren of the country's poorest people are going to live is a clear unquestionable scandal.

The Cecil Parkinson and Sarah Keays affair

Cecil Parkinson was a successful politician tipped for the very top of politics, a self-made millionaire who became Tory Party Chairman from 1981. He was a trusted right-hand man of Margaret Thatcher, and was credited with masterminding her 1983 General Election victory.

It was at the height of his career, at the time when it was thought he was about to be rewarded with the Foreign Secretary job, when he made a confession to Thatcher. Parkinson had got his House of Commons secretary Sarah Keays pregnant, after a twelve-year affair. He resigned his Cabinet post in October 1983. However, things seemed to go from bad to worse when fresh embarrassment appeared for Parkinson and new details emerged about his affair. Keays published a statement in *The Times* to put the record straight. In the statement she criticised her former lover's attitude towards her and the pregnancy and announced that she did not think her former lover had been frank and open about their relationship. She claimed he had proposed to her on a number of occasions, later changing his mind.

After the scandal, Keays went on to have a baby girl called Flora in December 1983. Parkinson went back to his wife Ann. The baby's identity was hidden by court order until she reached the age of eighteen. Flora herself was at the centre of a Channel 4 documentary and commented on how she missed knowing her dad. Meanwhile, Parkinson became Conservative Party Chairman once again, this time under William Hague's leadership, in 1997. He also became a life peer in the House of Lords.

Flora Keays has faced a number of challenges of her own over the years, having to deal with Asperger's Syndrome and suffering from fits. Before her fifth birthday she had a massive operation to remove a benign brain tumour, leaving her with learning difficulties. Despite this, Flora has worked as a volunteer in a children's nursery and was once nominated for a Young Person of the Year award in her home county of Gloucestershire. Her ambitions include learning to drive and attending a childcare course at college.

Tory MP Keith Hampson's brush with the law

In a case reminiscent of gay entrapment by police officers in 1960s' America, Tory MP Keith Hampson was trapped by undercover police officers at a Soho nightclub. The MP for Leeds North-West was parliamentary private secretary to Defence Secretary Michael Heseltine, and wrote many of his speeches.

On 3 May 1984, Hampson needed to kill some time before joining his wife that evening and wandered into the Gay Theatre in Berwick Street. The establishment showed male strippers. While he was there he spotted a woman nearby and was not sure if it was a real woman or a man in drag. After all, it was a busy, smoke-filled club, and quite difficult to make out. Hampson moved closer to take a look and as he did, he claimed that he accidentally brushed the thigh of a man standing next to him. The man, and the woman he was trying to look at, were police officers. Hampson was arrested for indecent assault, and later charged.

(Illustration by Bea Fox)

In court the male police officer made claims that his groin and buttocks had been touched, but Hampson had used the phrase 'accidentally brushed'. His wife testified that her husband was heterosexual, and he had a character witness in the form of Lord Tonypandy, who was a former Speaker of the House of Commons. However, the manager of the club said Hampson had been there a number of times.

The jury at Southwark Crown Court failed to reach a verdict. A retrial was deemed untenable because of the widespread publicity, according to Attorney General Sir Michael Havers. Throughout the case, Hampson was adamant that the charge against him was simply not true. His reputation was saved, he was innocent, but his seat was lost in 1997, when so many Tories lost their seats, because of the massive Labour Party landslide under Tony Blair.

Editing the miners' strike

Journalists can be as dodgy and scandalous as MPs, if not more so; I know, because I used to be one! One of the worst cases of manipulating the news for political self-gain was during the miners' strike of 1984-85. There have been a number of different accounts of the miners' strike from several angles over the years. The Freedom of Information Act 2000 has since revealed further details. Historians have mostly covered this event 'from the bottom up', as they call it. This includes accounts from individual, ordinary men and women involved in the action. This is in preference to another historical approach, focusing on the 'great men' involved. In other words, stories from the troops rather than the generals, or from the workers rather than the bosses.

The most interesting study of the strike came from Arthur Wakefield, a Yorkshire miner and 'accidental' historian who kept a diary of his striking activities. Naturally, it is only a one-sided account of his own personal experience. It is a straightforward narrative with little detail or political comment. It has a Brobdingnagian selection of primary source material, including sources from the Battle of Orgreave, 18 June 1984, one of the major events during the action. It is one particular news report in one long-running industrial action that I have chosen to mark as 'scandalous'. BBC coverage of Orgreave showed rioting and attacking miners and then police charging at them. In fact, it happened the other way round! The police attacked the miners and the miners fought back; incorrect editing completely distorted events. The BBC admitted an editing 'blunder'. Media historian Michael Bailey claims police in charge of the operation knew exactly what was happening. We must ask how much of this was ordered from above, politically, and whether it was a mistake or whether it was because Arthur Scargill hated the press. Whatever the answer, it was a scandalous piece of political journalism. However, if the press hated Scargill, it was surely his own fault. He referred to them as piranhas and liars, and there are plenty of stories of journalists being attacked at picket lines, many of whom were, of course, just doing their job!

One of the little-known but serious knock-on effects of the miners' strike was that the government of the day took its eye off the ball. This resulted in the bombing in October 1984 of the Grand Hotel in Brighton, where almost the entire government were staying during the Conservative Party conference. Five people died and many others were seriously injured. Security forces were expecting mass demonstrations in support of the miners, even in protest at the death of hunger striker Bobby Sands from years before, but not so much an IRA attack. Therefore, the search of the hotel prior to the conference was insufficient. According to the Hoddinott Report (a review into the Brighton bombing), not all the rooms were checked; that would have been impracticable, necessitating the closing of the entire building for weeks before the conference. If they had searched the hotel, perhaps they would have found the time bomb that had been planted weeks earlier under a bath panel in Room 629 by IRA member Patrick Magee. He had signed in as a guest using the false name of Roy Walsh.

With regard to the miners' strike, there are a number of scandals that should be considered, depending on which side of the political spectrum you sit. All these years after the event, many believe it was a scandal to close the pits and put so many men out of work, effectively paralysing the mining communities. Those on the other side of the spectrum will argue that it was a scandal that the unions had so much power post–Second World War, and that something had to be done to prevent losing so many working days to strike action.

The Merseyside MP who liked to party hard and be whipped even harder

The late Labour MP for Bootle, Allan Roberts, was known for three things: his left-wing views; his casual dress in the House of Commons; and his love of S&M. Allan Roberts was an MP from 1979 until his death in 1990. He was also a former teacher and social worker.

The fun-loving, party-going bachelor was known for his love of having a good time. He had once seriously upset his neighbours with his late-night partying. However, in 1981, *News of the World* and *Private Eye* carried stories about his trip to a Berlin gay nightclub in the city's red light district. The headlines made claims about gay sex romps, including whipping, men in SS uniforms and bondage. He accepted the claims at the time but refused to speak to the press about it.

Roberts said he had just been drunk and fallen over after claims that he had been whipped so hard he needed hospital treatment. A number of reporters had interviewed witnesses from the club to confirm Roberts' behaviour that night. There were claims that he had been dragged around the room, whipped and wore a dog collar. He was having a good time too, according to the witnesses. *Private Eye* also reported a time when Roberts had apparently been forced to keep his hand in his pocket in public because there was a handcuff attached to the wrist and a suggestion that the key had been lost.

In the 1980s, Roberts part-owned a pub called Lord Hood and along with his business partner tried to establish a music hall in the pub's function room. It was popular but not profitable. Overall, there was something about the man that his voters must have liked. At the time of his death he had a majority of more than 24,000, one of the biggest in the House of Commons. He was never outed as being gay, despite several attempts, and he never admitted a penchant for masochism, despite the stories surrounding his private life. He remained an active speaker, willing to defend gay rights. He became a successful member of the Labour government and frontbencher on environment. He had a reputation, not just as a party animal, but also as a kind and considerate man. He was well liked and respected. Sadly, he lost his fight against cancer at the early age of forty-six.

John Major and Edwina Currie – the affair the newspapers missed

It was almost like imagining your parents at it! John Major and Edwina Currie had a fling from 1984 to 1988. Despite Major launching the Back to Basics initiative in 1993 as Britain's prime minister, he was still not found out. The press was sniffing round for sleaze and scandal amongst the Tories when Major launched the campaign, which was based on traditional morality and family life. The press missed the big one; the major scandal. The prime minister had had an affair with Edwina Currie a few years earlier. The relationship carried on until John Major was promoted to the Cabinet. Amazingly, nobody knew about it even then. It may even have stayed top secret had it not been for the 2002 publication of Edwina Currie's diaries, which eventually gave the game away. She talked about a big man in his blue underpants!

The Tory MP who fed a beefburger to his daughter during the BSE crisis

Cast your mind back to May 1990, and the beef and BSE scare that gripped the nation. People were worried about whether or not beef was safe to eat. The government was desperate to reassure the general public that British beef was indeed completely safe. People had become worried about the spread of the disease in cattle and sales had fallen. Since the first case in 1986, it had grown to about 14,000 cases. Furthermore, there were fears that it could actually jump species and cause CJD, the human brain condition that is fatal. The link between eating beef and variant CJD was confirmed six years later. Schools started to take beef off the menu and France stopped all imports of British beef; other

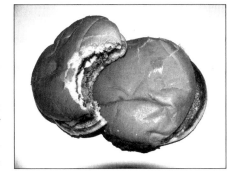

Beefburgers – with a bite taken out. (Bridget Hughes)

countries followed over the years. A blanket ban was not lifted until 2006. The beef industry was hit very hard, as selective culls were organised for the cattle that were labelled as most at risk.

The Minister of Agriculture, John Selwyn Gummer, invited the press to watch him and his 4-year-old daughter Cordelia tuck into a beefburger to reassure the general public. Unfortunately, the stunt backfired when his daughter refused to eat the burger and he was forced to chomp away on his own and declare to the media how lovely it tasted. Gummer's beef-chomping family performance at the Suffolk Boat Show on 16 May 1990 is the one single event he is remembered for. One could argue that it was a scandal to use his own child to reinforce his own political views. This historical blunder has even found its way into parliamentary slang: 'Doing a Gummer' is still used by politicians today. This weird event was not officially a scandal, and Gummer was not officially criticised for his stunt, indeed, remaining in John Major's Cabinet until the Conservatives lost power in 1997. David Clark, Labour's agriculture spokesman, used the word 'fiasco' to describe the government's handling of the BSE crisis. Sadly, the daughter of one of Mr Gummer's close friends died from the human form of mad cow disease in 2007.

Homes for votes scandal

This involved the selling off of council housing in the 1980s to potential Conservative voters. It centred on Westminster City Council. In 1986, the Conservative majority in the council had been reduced from twenty-six to four. The council, under Shirley Porter (the daughter of the Tesco founder Jack Cohen), implemented the Building Stable Communities policy, focusing on marginal wards. Homes were more likely to be sold to those in areas where more Conservative voters would be needed in the next local election. From 1987 to 1989, the housing policy was aimed at eight marginal wards in the borough, and properties were sold at a fraction of their market value.

Homeless people were allegedly moved out of the borough as they were seen as far less likely to vote

People's desire for their own home used as a political tool. (Kieran Hughes)

Conservative in the next election. In 1989, more than a hundred homeless families were removed from hostels in marginal wards. The manipulation of the electorate perhaps contributed to the 1990 Conservative victory in Westminster. By 1994, a number of people were being questioned as part of an investigation into these developments and Dr Michael Dutt, joint chairman of Westminster's housing committee (1988-90), was found dead from a self-inflicted gunshot wound with papers from the investigation by his side. Over the years there have been several investigations, judgements appeals, and more questions.

In the mid-1990s, Porter was found guilty of 'wilful misconduct' and 'disgraceful and improper gerrymandering'. Porter was pursued by the government for the millions of pounds that the cheap sales had cost the taxpayer. At one stage, Porter owed £42 million in surcharges for her part in the scandal and was ordered by the district auditor, John Magill, to pay the money, although that figure was later greatly reduced and Porter paid up. By 2009, the council publicly apologised and said it was the opposite of its policies today.

Handbags at dawn – did Thatcher and the Queen get on?

Traditionally the British prime minister and the country's monarch work in tandem; it's Her Majesty's government and so the queen (or king) is not supposed to have political opinions, or certainly not discuss them in public. A minor scandal occurred in July 1986, when *The Sunday Times* newspaper claimed that there was a rift between Her Majesty and Prime Minister Margaret Thatcher, quoting sources close to the Queen. It was reported that the Queen thought Thatcher was uncaring. The scandal was short-lived and soon calmed down but the thought that the Queen did not like the PM hung around for some time to come.

'Paddy Pantsdown' – Paddy Ashdown's affair

In 1992, the Lib-Dem leader Paddy Ashdown was given the rather embarrassing nickname Paddy Pantsdown. It followed his admission of a five-month affair with his personal secretary, Tricia Howard, five years earlier. Ashdown had confessed all to his lawyer, Andrew Phillips, in 1990, many years after the affair. Phillips had taken notes and placed them carefully in his safe but it was broken into and the notes were stolen and found their way to the tabloid newspapers. To defuse the situation, Ashdown called a press conference and confessed all, saying that it was all now in the past and that his wife had forgiven him. It meant that he did not have to resign his position.

Tricia Howard has repeatedly turned down huge sums of money to tell her side of the story, demonstrating some decency.

The Westland Helicopters affair

In 1986, the Thatcher government suffered one of its worst internal splits of its entire existence. The fallout was over the future of Westland Helicopters. It was the last British manufacturer of helicopters and its long-term future was in serious doubt. There had been a number of briefings and meetings over its future at Cabinet level. Defence Secretary Michael Heseltine and Prime Minister Margaret Thatcher could not see eye to eye over the issue. Heseltine favoured a link with a European consortium while Thatcher (and Westland itself) wanted to consider an American bid. Michael Heseltine did not like the fact that ministers had to first 'clear' public Westland comments through the Cabinet Office. He resigned and walked out of Downing Street. In 1990, Heseltine challenged Thatcher for the top job as leader of the party, but failed. It did, however, lead to Thatcher's downfall.

Michael Heseltine wrote about the Westland affair in his autobiography twelve years later and accused Thatcher of poisoning the political system, claiming that her actions had been an affront to the standards of government. In Grant Jordan's *The British Administrative System: Principles Versus Practice* he argues that post-Westland, Nigel Lawson's resignation also questioned the way things were done at Cabinet level in Thatcher's government.

Cabinet minister Norman Tebbit made it clear that Heseltine lacked support over the issue. Lord Tebbit is pictured here years later with the author of this book. (Kieran Hughes)

Lord Tebbit told *The Telegraph* that the account in Heseltine's *Life in the Jungle* was 'remote from the truth'. The former Tory Party chairman also said that Mr Heseltine himself was to blame for 'poisoning' relations between government colleagues, and insisted that when Michael Heseltine walked out, most of the Cabinet had failed to take his side. Lord Tebbit says Heseltine did not have Cabinet support over Westland.

Edwina Currie and the great egg scandal

In 1988, as Junior Health Minister, Edwina Currie dropped a clanger by incorrectly claiming that most of Britain's egg production was infected with the salmonella bacteria. The MP for South Derbyshire made the ridiculous remarks during an ITN television interview. Farmers, egg producers and certain politicians (especially some at the Ministry of Agriculture) were rather upset by her remarks. Her exact words were, 'Most of the egg production in this country, sadly, is now affected with salmonella.' Naturally, people panicked, and sales of eggs dramatically fell. Egg producers faced financial and operational difficulties. Sales fell 60 per cent overnight. Farmers had to slaughter 4 million hens as a result of the crisis and 400 million unwanted eggs had to be destroyed. Edwina Currie was left with egg on her face!

There was, of course, no evidence to support Edwina Currie's claims and the British Egg Industry Council took legal advice. It said that the risk of an egg being infected with salmonella was less than 200 million to one.

Edwina, left with egg on her face. (Illustration by Bea Fox)

There were claims that the National Farmers' Union was also seeking legal advice. The heat was on, and Currie eventually resigned from her position on 17 December. In Martin Hickman's article 'The Big Question: Was Edwina Currie right about salmonella in eggs, after all?' in *The Independent* (2006), he highlighted the higher salmonella levels in certain foreign eggs and also argued a positive that came out of Currie's egg crisis. He pointed out that salmonella levels in the late 1980s were indeed too high and that by making her comments, she had actually highlighted the problem, which was eventually solved by the use of vaccination. It was not just her comments about eggs that upset so many people. Edwina Currie had made a number of scandalous remarks in her early years in the public eye, upsetting many people. She said northerners were dying of ignorance and chips, old people should keep warm in the winter by wearing long johns and that good Christian people who would not dream of misbehaving would not catch AIDS. She had represented her South Derbyshire constituency since 1983. Then, in 1986, she was given the role of Junior Health Minister. She remained as an MP until the 1997 General Election, when she lost her seat. Since that time she has made a successful career for herself as a writer and broadcaster.

Edwina's scandalous remarks continued in October 2011 in a BBC Radio 5 Live phone-in during a conversation about the cost of heating and people being forced to choose between heating and food. The content and her manner towards some of those calling in to debate the issue with her was jaw-dropping. Currie said she did not believe people were starving in the United Kingdom and insisted it was a political argument, and that there were people really starving in the world, but not in the UK. Two listeners told her she was wrong and explained what was happening in the 'real world', but she argued with them. A professional carer who called in and told of her poverty said she also saw people in her line of work every day who do not have enough money to eat healthily.

Edwina Currie said to her: 'Are you telling me people in this country are going hungry?'

The caller replied, 'Absolutely.'

Currie said, 'Do you know, I really have great difficulty in believing that.'

Currie said she did not think people in this country go hungry, and asked if these 'starving people' were buying the odd lottery ticket or having the occasional cigarette. She asked, 'Somewhere along the line does food come as the first priority?'

A male caller told Edwina she was wrong, to which she replied, 'Oh really?' in a patronising manner. Amazingly, she continued by saying, 'I'd like to have some of these starving people in Britain produced; I say there's nobody starving in this country.' The male caller explained how he had to help out his mother so she could buy bread, and an unsympathetic Edwina Currie ranted on about how the issue is sometimes used politically and insisted that people in Britain do not go hungry. She vehemently insisted that there are no starving people in the United Kingdom.

In August 2012, during the opening of the Paralympic Games in London, when on Twitter Edwina Currie described the Italian Paralympians as 'gorgeous, even in wheelchairs'. People went crazy, calling her comments patronising, disgusting, ignorant, insensitive and offensive. She insisted it was just meant as a compliment and tweeted 'Get off with the patronising.' She simply failed to see how demeaning and mean her comments really were. Even if she did not mean it, she failed to listen to comments going on around her.

The Michael Mates resignation

This story is about the downfall of a Tory minister after a relationship with a businessman that seemed a scandal to many at the time. Michael Mates had done nothing wrong, but some thought his actions did not look good, and Mates himself resigned from the Major government on 24 June 1993.

Michael Mates had failed to succeed in the Thatcher years because he had strongly opposed the poll tax, but John Major appointed Mates as Northern Ireland Minister in 1992. His newfound success was short-lived because of his association with businessman Asil Nadir. Turkish-Cypriot Nadir was head of the Polly Peck empire. The textiles-to-packaging and electronics-to-food conglomerate seemed to be going from strength to strength as it grew throughout the 1980s. However, in 1990, it went bankrupt, with staggering debts of hundreds of millions of pounds. Nadir himself faced charges of theft and fled to Northern Cyprus. He was jailed in 2012, when he returned to Britain. Meanwhile, Nadir had had his watch confiscated by the authorities, and Mates had sent him a watch as a gift, bearing the inscription: 'Don't let the buggers get you down'. After this a letter came to light where Mates had complained to the Attorney General about the handling of the whole Nadir case. At the time, Major and Mates had seemed to get through the watch inscription scandal but in the end it led to Mates's resignation.

Dennis Skinner's love life

Dennis Skinner was a formidable political figure, a hardened socialist, from a coal-mining background, and proud of his working-class heritage. In 1994, the MP whom political sketch writers had nicknamed the 'Beast of Bolsover' was exposed as having a secret mistress, and given a new name, the 'Beast of Leg-over'. On 20 February, the *News of the World* ran the headline: 'Commons Mr Angry has Secret Mistress. The Beast of Leg-over'. It sold more copies than usual in his home village of Clay Cross, Derbyshire.

It emerged that Dennis Skinner had been having a relationship with his Commons researcher, Lois Blasenheim. Skinner had been meeting her at her small Chelsea flat, in disguise, according to some of the newspapers. The scandal was a welcome break for the Conservative government, which had suffered some bad publicity. Married Skinner, who had never shied away from saying what he thought, got a bit of stick from MPs in the House, and many Tory MPs who had suffered from sharp-tongued Skinner in the past, got their revenge. Skinner had effectively been separated from his wife for some time, but his rivals didn't see that as an excuse.

David Mellor and the Chelsea strip fling

This was an almost comedic and tragic exit from politics, as Conservative Cabinet Minister David Mellor was exposed as having an affair with the Spanish actress Antonia de Sancha. Certain tabloids had wrongly said that Mellor had made love in his beloved Chelsea strip and sucked her toes. Both of these were untrue, making David Mellor an object of ridicule. The affair was featured in most newspapers and Antonia de Sancha seemed to be on every television and radio station. Mellor insisted he had the backing of the prime minister. There were more serious allegations ahead – of free holidays, courtesy of the daughter of a PLO supporter. David Mellor had become an embarrassment to the prime minister, John Major, and to the government. Therefore he quit his Cabinet post, and eventually lost his parliamentary seat, like so many Tories, on the night of the 1997 Labour landslide. David Mellor tried to remain dignified and professional to the end, offering his opponent a magnanimous concession speech, despite being slow-clapped out of office by a rude crowd amid chants of 'Out! Out! Out!'

Mellor might have been laughed at for his affair, but he had the last laugh when he went on to become a successful broadcaster, including having his own show on London's LBC Radio, where he turned out to be a most talented on-air performer, at one point teaming up with former London Mayor Ken Livingstone to do an on-air serious double act.

The Formula One sponsorship scandal

There was once a time when cigarette and tobacco advertising was everywhere. In recent times though, and in many places, it has all but disappeared, along with smoking in public buildings. In 1997, when Tony Blair's New Labour was high in the polls and on its way to defeating the tired Conservatives who had been in power since 1979, campaigners promised to support a ban on tobacco company sponsorship and advertising. The ban was part of a European Union directive. However, in the UK, Formula One was unhappy about the move as most of its teams were sponsored by tobacco companies. The head of Formula One Management, Bernie Ecclestone, met government representatives after the election victory and got an exemption from the ban for Formula One. Had some backroom deal been done; some old boys' handshake? Several newspapers smelled a rat and starting investigating the exemption. They found that Ecclestone had donated £1 million to the Labour Party. Tony Blair could not afford this type of scandal so soon after getting into office and returned the money before making a public apology. Blair denied that the exemption had anything to do with Ecclestone's meeting with officials.

An 'error of judgement' by Ron Davies

When the Labour Party enjoyed its massive landslide in 1997, Ron Davies became Secretary of State for Wales. However, things went drastically wrong for Mr Davies after he was caught up in what he described as an 'error of judgement'. His actions prompted his resignation in 1998. He had apparently met a man on Clapham Common, which is a well-known gay pick-up place. Davies claimed that he had agreed to join the man for dinner, later meeting up with another man and a woman. As they drove to Brixton, the three people apparently turned on Davies and robbed him. Davies has always denied that the meeting had anything to do with drugs or sex. Later, he told reporters that he had paid a very high price for this incident. Years later, in 2003, he was elected to the Welsh Assembly but faced allegations of visiting a well-known gay cruising spot. He claimed he was badger-watching. This allegation was enough to make Davies stand down, and this time to resign from the Labour Party in 2004.

'Two Shags!' John Prescott's affair

Throughout Britain's Blairite years, John Prescott served as the country's deputy prime minister, with respected links to the working class. He served as MP for East Hull from 1970, right through to 2010. In 2006, he admitted having an affair.

At the age of sixty-seven, he said he had had a two-year liaison with his secretary, Tracey Temple, who was more than twenty years younger than him. He announced that it was something he had regretted, and that his wife Pauline was devastated by the news. Some of the tabloid journalists mimicked him by altering his well-known nickname of 'Two Jags' to 'Two Shags'!

The Robin Cook affair

Shadow Foreign Secretary Robin Cook's affair was almost ignored and definitely overshadowed by the Tory sleaze of the 1990s. But it was a very different story when Labour took power in 1997. Suddenly, the press took much more of an interest in Mr Cook's private life. The *News of the World* contacted Downing Street on a Friday about running the story about Robin Cook that weekend. Blair's press man, Alastair Campbell, told Cook that his affair was about to be splashed all over the Sunday newspapers. Cook was at an airport transferring flights when he received the call, while trying to enjoy a holiday with his wife. He cancelled the rest of the trip and within twenty-four hours had made an announcement that he was leaving his wife to be with his mistress, Gaynor Regan, whom he later married; she was also his secretary. In her own book, serialised in a national newspaper, Cook's wife went into great detail about their troubled love life, speaking openly. Her book, *A Slight and Delicate Creature*, was a complete embarrassment for Robin. She described him as cold and unfeeling, but also revealed what he thought about his colleagues. The book claimed Robin Cook was jealous of Gordon Brown and hated Peter Mandelson.

The long-term effect on Cook's political life will never really be known. On 6 August 2005, at the age of fifty-nine, Robin Cook collapsed and died while out walking in the hills of Scotland with his wife Gaynor.

In Tony Blair's post-2001 election victory re-shuffle, Cook was demoted to become Leader of the Commons, replaced at the Foreign Office by Jack Straw. He quit his post as Commons Leader in March 2003 in protest over the war in Iraq. Outside government, he had been an active rebel and remained a vocal critic of Tony Blair's foreign policy from the backbench. He could not have ever hoped for a return in a Brown-led Labour government, as the two had been arch-enemies for almost thirty years.

How things went wrong for David Blunkett

Here was a man who lost so much through scandal. He was a successful politician, having got the big promotion after Tony Blair's 2001 victory, taking him from Education Secretary to Home Secretary, with talk of him being a future prime minister. He had emerged from a challenging background, having lost his father at an early age and having been born blind.

In August 2004, the press revealed the story about Blunkett's relationship with a married woman, Kimberly Quinn, editor of *The Spectator*. In November 2004, he was accused of using his position to fast-track a visa application for Quinn's nanny, which he denied. Just when he thought it could not get any worse, embarrassing criticisms he had apparently made of his colleagues emerged from his biographer. Blunkett quit, even before the inquiry into whether or not he had fast-tracked the visa got under way. Blunkett did make a surprising return to a Cabinet position in 2005, but this only lasted a few months because of a new incident. This time, questions were asked about him taking a directorship at DNA Bioscience, and why he had not consulted an advisory committee, which would have been normal practice for ex-ministers. Blunkett decided to step down.

Euan Blair raises a glass or three to the new anti-drink initiative

Lots of teenagers experiment with alcohol – a sip of beer at an older friend's house, a vodka at Christmas, perhaps. How about the prime minister's 16-year-old son drinking way too much and then throwing up all over Leicester Square in London? That would be bad enough at sixteen, as well as being the son of the then Prime Minister Tony Blair. However, it got much worse than that. A fun-packed night in July 2000 is one that Euan Blair would probably prefer to forget. He was arrested for being drunk; bad enough. But his father had just announced a new initiative of getting drunks frogmarched to cash point machines to pay on-the-spot fines for their drunken behaviour in the street.

And it did not end there. Just as Euan Blair had already embarrassed his father enough, he decided to give police a false name and address. His real identity was soon discovered when he was searched. It turned out not to be the best day for the Blairs.

Leicester Square. (Kevin Taylor)

Punching Prescott

Some political scandals make you shake your head in disapproval, others make you angry or shocked, and some, like this one, make you want to laugh out loud. In 2001, the then Labour Deputy Prime Minister John Prescott was on an election walkabout in Rhyl, North Wales. A man called Craig Evans decided to be a bit of a protestor – or, in some people's eyes, a yob – and hurled an egg at Prescott. Not the usual reaction from a senior politician, but Mr Prescott thumped the protestor right in the head.

I suspect many people were cheering on John Prescott throughout the whole incident. Prescott claimed self-defence because the protesting farm worker had thrown the egg first and thus avoided any legal action. The punch was repeated over and over again on channels such as Sky News. 'Two Jags' became known as 'Two Jabs'.

When is it a good day to bury bad news?

In September 2001, Labour Party aide Jo Moore realistically ended her career in politics by writing just one badly-worded memo. Moore worked for Stephen Byers, the Secretary of State for Transport, Local Government and the Regions. In response to terrorists flying planes into New York's Twin Towers, Moore's memo stated: 'It is now a very good day to get out anything we want to bury.' Shortly afterwards, the towers collapsed, burying thousands of innocent victims. It was spin, but not as we knew it! This time it was in really bad taste. The prime minister's spokesperson referred to it as a serious error of judgement. There was an outcry at Moore's comments and she made an apology. She received a formal reprimand. Her boss Stephen Byers decided that that was enough and stood by her. There was growing pressure for her to go but she stayed for some months. In February 2002, the BBC's online political correspondent Nyta Mann described her unpopularity by reporting that 'a formidable array of voices was assembled in coalition against her remaining in post.'

The following February, Jo Moore was accused of planning

(Kieran Hughes)

to release bad railway statistics on the day of Princess Margaret's funeral, although she claimed the dates had been suggested before the funeral was planned. The details of this were leaked to the press and found their way onto the front pages. Within days, Moore and her immediate superior both resigned. She claimed that some people had been inventing stories about her. Moore went on to train as a primary school teacher.

The 1996 Arms-to-Iraq scandal

In the 1980s, Saddam Hussein's regime in Iraq purchased a UK machine tools company called Matrix Churchill. The company was selling weapon components to Iraq, its directors ended up in court as a result, and the case collapsed. A special inquiry was set up as a result and the scandal was reported in newspapers, and on television and radio worldwide. It revealed the government's secrecy, underhandedness, dishonesty and stupidity.

In 1991, Britain went to war with Iraq over its invasion of Kuwait. After the war there was a lot of interest over whether British companies had been supplying Saddam Hussein with equipment that might have benefitted his regime and be used against his enemies. In 1992, three of Matrix Churchill's directors were put on trial for selling equipment to Iraq. Eventually the trial collapsed after it was revealed that Matrix Churchill had in fact been advised by the government over its sales to Iraq. British defence chiefs had even been helping the company get the necessary export licences, but they had tried to keep this quiet. The Scott Inquiry, conducted by Sir Richard Scott, then a Lord Justice of Appeal, took up the reins and analysed what had actually happened. Former Trade and Defence Minister Alan Clark told the Scott Inquiry that a decision to prosecute the three Matrix Churchill businessmen was 'ludicrous' and said he could see no justification for the trial.

In 1996, after three years, the report of Sir Richard Scott's inquiry was finally published. It contained strong criticisms of ministers involved in the scandal. Several senior personnel were named and shamed. The report also strongly criticised the government for not telling Parliament of reforms to arms export laws, because it had been worried about a possible public outcry. The export of non-lethal military goods had been eased after the Iran-Iraq ceasefire in 1988. The weapon makers had been taken to court for attempting to export arms without parliamentary permission, although it emerged later that in fact Matrix *did* have the right authority under up-to-date regulations. It also became apparent that the government had been aware of the exports to Iraq all along.

The Arms-to-Iraq scandal also brought the sensitive issue of public interest immunity (PII) to the public's attention. PII is the process of keeping highly sensitive information out of the public domain, for matters of national security, for example. As a result, the whole question of openness was raised.

Mark Oaten's sex scandal

Liberal Democrat Mark Oaten was in line for a glittering political career until he messed it up in glorious style in 2004. He had first won his parliamentary seat in the 1997 General Election.

Initially, he had got through on a majority of 'two', but a re-run saw him get through by more than 21,000 votes. By 2003, he was Lib Dem Home Affairs spokesman. The future looked rather rosy for a man thought to be a party leader in waiting. However, the married Oaten starting seeing a rent boy, who was twenty-three years old. In January 2006, he decided to run for the party leadership, and the *News of the World* told him that they knew all about his relationship from 2004. Oaten resigned from the leadership race because of a lack of support. The *News of the World* ran the story and described Oaten taking part in a 'bizarre sex act'. There were tales and allegations of three-in-a-bed. As *The Spectator* put it, it had to have been the only time the *Sunday Telegraph* mentioned the act of coprophilia in its discussion pages. Oaten blamed his hair loss on the whole affair. He also said he was trying to undermine his career on purpose, which would have been easier than actually resigning from the front bench himself. He said it was a private nightmare and a public scandal.

The 'Wicked Witch of the North'

A former councilor, mayor and Northern Ireland Assembly member and MP caused a scandal in 2008 with her anti-gay comments in a radio interview. Iris Robinson claimed gay people could be 'turned around' with help. The content was bad enough but the timing was almost as bad. It was the week that a gay man had been beaten in a homophobic attack. There was outrage at her comments and 16,000 people signed a petition calling for Prime Minister Gordon Brown to reprimand Mrs Robinson.

There was even a police investigation following her comments, as they breached hate crime laws. No charges were brought against her though. Gay rights groups gave her the title 'Bigot of the Year' in 2008, and another group dubbed her 'Wicked Witch of the North'. In December 2009, Mrs Robinson announced that she was quitting politics after declaring that the stress of public office had taken its toll. She announced that she had been battling problems with mental illness.

Naughty MP gets fresh in the House of Commons

In news and politics, timing is important. Put the two together, and timing is absolutely crucial. This is evident in the case of Nigel Griffiths MP. In March 2009, the *News of the World* ran a story about the married Member of Parliament for Edinburgh South being caught in a tryst with a brunette in his office at the House of Commons. He denied being unfaithful to his wife. The newspapers managed to print some pictures of the encounter, which included a brunette's leg in stockings peeping out from behind a door.

What made this scandal even worse was the fact that it happened on Remembrance Day. It was not something that went down particularly well with many people. This was the kind of story that would run and run from every angle, with a tabloid endeavour to get more photos and dirt, no doubt. But Griffiths was saved by the bell … in fact, by the Home Secretary's husband. A week later, after Griffiths was getting it for real, Home Secretary Jacqui Smith's husband was watching porn on his TV and charging it to the taxpayer. Fleet Street, the general public and almost everyone else was more interested in this huge embarrassment than in just another MP being naughty. Griffiths' misdemeanor was reduced to a few lines in the newspapers.

The Great British parliamentary expenses scandal

In 2009, some of Britain's top politicians were caught out claiming for things they simply should not have been claiming for on their expense accounts. Some of these items were claimed for in error, others not (and they were dealt with by the courts), and above all, even those claims that were legal and legitimate, where MPs had done nothing wrong, raised the nation's eyebrows. 'You are legally allowed to claim for what?' asked many. The British public was outraged to hear what they, the taxpayers, had been paying for over the years.

The list included items and services from duck pond maintenance to flat-screen TVs, from pornographic films to mortgages on second homes, including those where the mortgage had been paid off. The end result was a new code of conduct, new rules, and in some cases conviction and imprisonment. The scandal included backbenchers, senior politicians and members of the House of Lords. Allegations were being thrown all over the place and an embarrassed Parliament was having to answer for every single penny of expenses. To make matters worse, it was at a time of recession, when normal people were watching every penny and pound, and the press was announcing new cases of wasting money on silly expenses and unnecessary luxuries.

Certain hypocritical MPs were lining their pockets with taxpayers' money and crying that they were playing by the rules. But the country was demanding refunds from the worst cases, and they got them. Some very large cheques were presented to the Treasury. The BBC TV programme *Question Time*, which dedicated a show to the scandal, had its highest ratings for thirty years. The audience was angry and some of the politicians were booed.

Some of the developments of the expenses scandal

January 2008:
The Information Commissioner ordered the House of Commons to release details of expenses claimed by just six MPs. They included Prime Minister Gordon Brown and his predecessor, Tony Blair. Then MP Derek Conway was found to have 'misused' expenses to employ his son and was forced to apologise.

February 2008:
The Commons was forced by the Information Tribunal to release expenses details of fourteen MPs.

March 2008:
This month saw the publication of the controversial 'John Lewis list' that showed how MPs could spend thousands of pounds on kitchens, TVs, bathrooms etc.

April 2008:
The argument over MPs employing relatives resulted in a new scheme where they now have to register exactly who is on their relatives' payroll.

May 2008:
In its constant battle to keep expenses a secret, the House of Commons lost its High Court battle against their disclosure.

February 2009:
The Home Secretary Jacqui Smith defended claiming allowances for a second home while she was residing with her sister.

March 2009:
The Committee on Standards in Public Life declared an inquiry into expenses would report after the next general election. Meanwhile, Jacqui Smith's husband apologised after an expenses claim mistakenly included adult movies that he had watched.

May 2009:
The *Daily Telegraph* newspaper published a series of further expenses details in relation to second homes claims, supposedly from a leaked computer disc. A number of MPs were named in the 'flipping' scandal, where they changed their second home to maximise claims and avoid capital gains tax. On behalf of the House, Prime Minister Gordon Brown publicly apologised to the country for the expenses scandal and David Cameron apologised on behalf of his MPs. One of the most bizarre expenses claims was that of Sir Peter Viggers, the MP for Gosport, Hampshire, who submitted an invoice for a 5-foot-high floating duck house for his pond, at a cost of more than £1,600. The MP of twenty-five years had claimed more than £30,000 of taxpayers' money for 'gardening' over three years. Ironically, he had also claimed £500 for 28 tons of manure!

June 2009:
This was a busy summer month that firstly saw Jacqui Smith announce that she would step down as Home Secretary as the next reshuffle. Sir Christopher Kelly accused MPs of exploiting expenses for personal gain, when he opened the first evidence meeting of the Committee on Standards in Public Life. MPs' expenses claims were published by the House of Commons, but there was outrage when many details were simply blacked out. Finally, Scotland Yard announced that a number of MPs and peers faced criminal investigations over their expenses claims.

October 2009:
Prime Minister Gordon Brown said he would repay more than £12,000 and encouraged other ministers to follow his example.

November 2009:
Commons Leader Harriet Harman said that she thought it unfair to make MPs sack their husbands and wives, after the recommendation on a ban on using taxpayers' money to employ spouses.

Jacqui Smith and the porn movies

This must be the ultimate humiliation for a politician; partner caught charging porn films to the taxpayer. At any time this would have looked bad but it was 2009, and MPs' expenses were under the spotlight. Politicians had to explain what they were claiming for all over again. The then Home Secretary Jacqui Smith held her head up in a dignified fashion and her husband, Richard

An embarrassing moment for the Smiths. (Illustration by Bea Fox)

Timney, also made a public apology. It seemed like a genuine error. Timney said he understood why people might be angry after two adult films were viewed at his home and mistakenly claimed for on expenses. Jacqui Smith repaid the money as quickly as she could and was up-front and honest about the error.

At the time, the Home Secretary was already being questioned over her use of the second homes allowance. She had been criticised for claiming taxpayer-funded allowances for a second home while living with her sister. Meanwhile, she issued a statement which said, 'I'm sorry that in claiming for my internet connection, I mistakenly claimed for a television package alongside it.' In reality, she was fighting for survival. The timing of her humiliation, coming just days before the arrival of the G20 leaders, was unfortunate and embarrassing. She was seen by some as a hypocrite, having previously criticised men who pay for sexual entertainment as she tightened up laws relating to lap dancing clubs. She had become the first woman Home Secretary when appointed in June 2007 and the second youngest ever (aged forty-four), after Winston Churchill. But this episode was bound to affect her perilously low constituency majority in Redditch of just 2,700; the smallest of all Cabinet members.

More expenses scandals …

It was not just some of Britain's MPs using their expenses in a questionable manner: some of New Zealand's MPs have also been accused in the past of misusing funds for various perks, including porn movies, trips abroad, massages, golf clubs and good food, all at the taxpayer's expense.

Meanwhile, in 2011, a South African politician was accused of spending in excess of the equivalent of £42,000 on travel and hotel bills, partly to fund a visit to a girlfriend jailed in Switzerland for drug smuggling.

Gordon Brown embarrasses himself

This was another slip-up of huge proportions, with the British prime minister criticising a voter in the run-up to the general election – and it was broadcast to the whole world! It was April 2010 when Gordon Brown was, in effect, fighting for his political life. Most knew that he had a slim chance of winning the election, and that was without any embarrassing slip-ups. Brown needed everything to go his way and a good wind behind him to stand any chance at all. However, if you are going to mess up, do it in style, why don't you! On a visit to a community re-offender project in Rochdale, 65-year-old Gillian Duffy (who had only popped out to buy a loaf of bread) called out to the prime minister to ask him why he was not dealing with the crisis of the national debt. One of his aides ushered the woman to the PM so that they could discuss the issue properly, as the TV cameras were rolling.

Mrs Duffy proceeded to politely ask about a number of issues such as the national debt and immigration. She was a force to be reckoned with and started a heated discussion with the prime minister. Gordon Brown was professional at the time and stayed polite and remained calm, smiling and tried to put his point forward, despite it being a rather uncomfortable incident. On the subject of immigration, for example, he explained that many British people go to work abroad in the same way that many come to Britain to work. This was in response to Mrs Duffy's comments about lots of immigrants coming to work in Britain.

The error occurred when Brown was driven away in his car and started complaining about the woman. He seemed anxious and angry and called her a 'bigoted woman' and complained that he should never have had to talk to her at all. Unfortunately, what Gordon Brown did not realise was that a Sky News microphone he was wearing for the walkabout was actually still turned on and picking up what he thought were his private words about Gillian Duffy. Of course, Sky News broadcast Brown's words and they were repeated by all the other news channels. Mrs Duffy, a former council worker, went about her business totally unaware of the chaos that had developed around the incident. Soon after the conversation TV camera crews and newspaper/radio reporters arrived at her house and it became the big story of the day. The 65-year-old did not understand why she had been verbally attacked by Gordon Brown after he had left the scene.

An embarrassed Brown had to face the music and apologise to Gillian Duffy. In addition to that, in fairness to the prime minister, he actually visited Duffy at her house to apologise face to face. He stayed there for forty-three minutes. Gordon Brown insisted that he was 'mortified' by his comments and said that he had simply misunderstood what Mrs Duffy had said to him. Mrs Duffy, however, refused to shake his hand and said that she might not even vote at all. TV crews were, of course, waiting outside the house for his comments. Soon afterwards, he lost the election and stood down from office.

Chapter Two

United States of America

American political treatment of the gay community

Most reasonable, sane people in this day and age will agree that the gay community has endured a long struggle over the years, in many countries, and still does to an extent. Historically, it is interesting to see how two countries in particular have treated homosexuals so badly – the United States and the United Kingdom. As a straight man researching this, it is difficult to comprehend how and why the gay community has been treated so badly. Starting with the United States, let us look at the politically scandalous way that gay men and women have been treated and how they have fought back. It is amazing that so much of this happened so recently; medieval behaviour in the twentieth century.

We should start a little earlier though, with President Thomas Jefferson (b.1743 d.1826), and his call in 1776 for legislation for gay men to be castrated as a punishment for their behaviour. Fast-forward to 1924, and the creation of the Society for Human Rights in Chicago, the country's earliest known gay rights organisation, which stated its aim was to 'protect the interests of people who by reasons of mental and physical abnormalities are abused and hindered in the legal pursuit of happiness.' This was a brave mission statement for its time! The society published the first American publication for homosexuals. It was called *Friendship and Freedom*. The society did not last very long. It disbanded after continual political pressure.

From the 1940s, the rights of homosexuals and the voice of this sexual minority grew in strength. This was a time of reform, with the emergence of the American Civil Rights Movement, demands for equality for women and the right to express one's sexuality. Later, in the 1950s and 1960s, gay and lesbian political movements flourished, with sexuality becoming more politicised. There were 'three Ps' of the gay community: plight, persecution and prejudice. They also suffered police raids, intimidation and discrimination.

In 1948, Alfred Kinsey published his report *Sexual Behaviour in the Human Male*, claiming homosexuality was more common than had been previously thought. He said around 37 per cent of adult males had had some homosexual

Thomas Jefferson, United States 3rd President, who proposed laws that would see gay men castrated.
(Illustration by Bea Fox)

experience, and that 10 per cent of men had spent at least three years being 'exclusively' gay. Many disagreed and disapproved of his research. Many psychologists and psychiatrists still argued that homosexuality was a form of illness. There was a 'cure' or 'punish' mentality.

Later, the advent of the Second World War was a catalyst for social upheaval, in terms of race, gender and sexuality. Everything was turned upside down during this time. There was a radical change in attitudes where one's race, sex or sexuality could affect political views. From the Second World War onwards, there was a moral battle between homosexuals and the government. During the war, women's military organisations such as the Navy WAVES and the WACS tested for sexual deviancy and often rooted out 'manly' women. In the semi-autobiographical *The Beautiful Room is Empty*, Edmund White recalls being thrown out of the United States Army for ticking the 'homosexual tendencies' box. The army doctor asked him if he had tried psychiatric treatment for it. Meanwhile, homosexuals were punished even *after* serving their country in the armed forces. The 1944 GI Bill prevented gay personnel from taking post-service benefits. Margot Canaday, in *Building a Straight State*, said federal policy explicitly excluded gays and lesbians from the economic benefits of the welfare state during this mid-century repression. Although this was a deliberate anti-gay policy, actually the structure of the welfare state was family orientated, and thus by its fundamental structure was pro-family, therefore pro-heterosexual. The discriminatory policy backfired though, because many closet homosexuals in the army kept quiet and claimed the benefits anyway.

The US government's scandalous behaviour towards the gay community did not stop at the military. On the quiet, at the start of the Cold War, government officials had been secretly investigating employees' sexual orientation. A Senate report entitled *Employment of Homosexuals and Other Sex Perverts in Government* was distributed to members of Congress. It declared homosexuals as suffering from mental illness and of being a major security risk. It decided that 'those who engage in overt acts of perversion lack the emotional stability of normal persons.' This 'Lavender Scare', as it became known, saw gay people as potential blackmail victims. This scare was as bad as the communist Red Scare and led to the sacking of many government personnel. Things were worse in Florida, where a war on 'perverts' was created, resulting in a mass exodus. Gay bars were routinely closed down, and there was a campaign to sack gay teachers. From 1950 onwards, civil service sackings continued and President Eisenhower issued Executive Order 10450, banning all sexual 'perverts' from government employment.

The employment discrimination followed intimidation in the gay bars, with undercover police trapping suspected gay men and women, and in military towns and ports, the US Army and Navy also patrolled the gay areas during and just after the war. They banned personnel from frequenting bars associated with homosexuality. Under the 1941 May Act, the military could shut them down. This gave the police confidence to constantly raid bars. In Nan Alamilla Boyd's *Wide-Open Town: A History of Queer San Francisco to 1965*, Joe Baron talks about police entrapment in San Francisco in the 1950s, being groped by undercover police and how gay people would sometimes be put on the Deviants Register (like the Sex Offenders Register in the UK).

So who was fighting back in the gay community? There were some key organisations, events and incidents. In 1950 in Los Angeles, the Mattachine Society was founded by gay rights activist Harry Hay. It was the first national gay rights organisation, based on an outspoken civil rights leadership style, surviving in separate cells. It wanted to 'eliminate discrimination, derision, prejudice and bigotry'. It believed homosexuals should be allowed to mix freely in mainstream society and be accepted for who they are. Some consider this to be the start of the gay rights movement in America.

It was followed by the launch of *ONE*, the first pro-gay magazine, sold openly on the streets of Los Angeles. The union of gay rights campaigners began to strengthen the cause. It was continued in 1955, when the lesbian group Daughters of Bilitis formed in San Francisco to work for the acceptance of lesbians in society. By the mid-1960s, gay people in the US were forming more visible groups and whole communities, as a basis for influencing radical social change. Many groups arranged sit-ins, strikes, pickets and protests over discrimination. The right for freedom of choice and privacy became a key social and political issue.

The famous court case Stoumen vs Reilly was also a turning point for gay rights. In 1949, San Francisco's Black Cat restaurant was accused of serving gays, and was raided and shut down. Its owner argued that gay people had a right to gather. Initial court hearings backed the authorities, but it went as high as California's Supreme Court in 1951, which ruled that gays were human beings and had a right to gather. It said homosexuality remained illegal, but the actual gathering of homosexuals was not illegal. The Black Cat got back its liquor licence. After the ruling, police policy on gay bars changed and it was more relaxed. Gay bars openly flourished, and changed from bars that welcomed gays into actual gay bars. In 1955, new laws allowed increased intimidation and surveillance under the Alcoholic Beverage Control Board. San Francisco changed from being a wide-open town with a sexual sub-culture to a town hostile to the gay community.

In the 1950s, American psychologist Evelyn Hooker widely wrote on the subject of homosexuality and administered several psychological tests on straight and gay men, concluding that gay and straight men are not that different and that homosexuality is not a clinical entity. This influential research did much to change people's views, but the government was still largely anti-gay and homosexuality was still illegal.

In 1969, the Stonewall riots turned isolated gay rights campaigns into a unified and widespread organisation demanding equal rights. Customers in the New York gay bar The Stonewall Inn fought back during a police raid, sparking three days of rioting in opposition to continued police persecution. Hundreds of people got involved. The bar had been raided time and time again, with police keen to rid the community of 'sexual deviants'. The significance of the riots was great. They influenced gay rights campaigners on a national level. Just days after Stonewall, many local gay rights groups were formed to join the fight against discrimination.

Even the quieter campaign groups were spurred on to organise new marches and events to further their cause. Stonewall brought the seriousness of the situation to the forefront of politics and social discussion. In 1969 after Stonewall, the Gay Liberation Front (GLF) was created out of several gay rights movements, becoming an influential organisation in the fight to promote rights for homosexuals. In its demand for equality and an end to gender roles it was seen as a strong force fighting for its rights. Supporters claimed the GLF increased the visibility of gay men and women, furthering their cause with great vigour. It is credited with creating a better public awareness of the link between homosexuality and politics.

However, lawmakers at state and federal level continued to target lesbians and gay men with draconian legislation and hateful rhetoric. Some progress was made in 1962, when Illinois became the first state to decriminalise homosexual acts in private, between consenting adults. Gay rights continued its struggle after 1970, with Harvey Milk becoming the first ever openly gay, publicly elected official on the San Francisco Board of Supervisors. After that came the struggle to fight Proposition 6.

Proposition 6

In the 1970s there seemed to be a huge increase in the number of gay people 'coming out'. This unnerved a lot of straight people. One of them was Californian State Senator John Briggs, who responded by trying to keep openly gay people and their supporters from working in public schools. He introduced Proposition 6 to the state ballot as proposed legislation to do this. He argued that gay people would be bad role models for young people. This was a direct political attack on gay people of both sexes. There were angry debates all over the state and gay issues were at the top of the political agenda for the first time.

The newly elected politician on the San Francisco Board of supervisors, Harvey Milk, came out fighting against Proposition 6, becoming its political opponent. He had only recently been elected to the board, making him the first openly gay politician in California to be elected to office. He argued against it over and over again, explaining why it should never be allowed. Milk had a lot of support and in November 1978, Proposition 6 was defeated.

His furious opponent, former supervisor Dan White, fatally shot Harvey Milk at City Hall. He also shot and killed Mayor George Moscone. Fifty thousand people with lighted candles took to the streets of San Francisco. The website tellingpictures.com (on its page about the 1984 film *The Times of Harvey Milk*), says that the Proposition 6 campaign was only one manifestation of anti-gay beliefs as gay men and women found their rightful place. Harvey Milk's murder was another. In May 1978, Dan White received a minimum seven-year sentence for 'involuntary manslaughter'. As a result, riots broke out in front of City Hall. White was released in 1983 and committed suicide in 1985.

Harvey Milk

Milk (b.1930 d.1978) became an icon in San Francisco and a martyr of the gay community. In 2009, he was posthumously awarded the Presidential Medal of Freedom. Gay rights and gay identities emerged and flourished as a result of events like Stonewall and from several anti-discriminatory Supreme Court decisions. Harvey Milk's victory over Proposition 6, the removal of homosexuality from the list of mental disorders in 1973 and tolerance in the military all contributed to an eventual acceptance and equality.

The Supreme Court in Washington, where several key rulings have helped the rights of gay citizens.
(Phil Seaman)

Two recent examples

1996: Romer vs Evans ruled against the state of Colorado, which wanted to deny gays and lesbians protection against discrimination.
2003: Lawrence vs Texas, the Court puts an end to legislation that criminalised same-sex intercourse.

There were also a number of examples at State judicial level.

The president's marriage

Rachel Donelson was born in Virginia in 1767 and came to Tennessee with her parents when she was twelve. At seventeen, she married a man called Lewis Robards, but it did not work out and they soon separated. She later heard that he was filing a petition for divorce.

A few years down the line, before being elected as president of the United States, Andrew Jackson married Rachel, in 1791. They both believed that she was legally divorced but they had made an honest mistake. In fact, Robards had sought permission to file for divorce but it had not completed. Andrew and Rachel suffered nasty whispers about adultery and bigamy, despite it only being a technical error. Robards then brought a case of adultery and eventually the divorce went through.

The Jacksons remarried in 1794, but the error was brought up and used against Andrew in the election of 1828. He was very quick to defend his wife's honour and she became a well-respected woman. Throughout their marriage and Andrew Jackson's military, business and political career, Rachel mostly stayed at their home at the Hermitage Plantation. The scandal had made Rachel withdraw somewhat, but she was present to support her husband's move into politics. Jackson blamed Rachel's early death on the many personal attacks against him. She was buried at the Hermitage, Nashville, Tennessee, on Christmas Eve in 1828.

Andrew and Rachel remained happily married. (Illustration by Bea Fox)

Thomas Jefferson and Sally Hemings – hidden love or false rumours?

Historians have never agreed on whether or not this US president kept his own personal concubine. At the time there was a rumour that he was having sex with his personal slave, Sally Hemings, after his wife had passed away. There was a rumour that he even fathered six children by Hemings. The subject has been discussed, researched and debated for two centuries. Through complex inter-slave/owner breeding, Sally was said to be an illegitimate half-sister of Jefferson's wife.

Opponents of Jefferson tended to agree that he had had the relationship and fathered these children. In 1802, one of his former allies, James T. Callender, turned journalist and reported the story to a local newspaper. Callender was an office seeker himself and had a number of professional issues with Jefferson. The president kept a dignified silence after the story was published. He made no official response. Over time, Jefferson's children and grandchildren denied the story and said it went against his moral grounds. The story was sustained throughout the nineteenth century by his critics. Modern-day DNA testing in 1998 on some of his alleged descendants proved persuasive, but not definitive. The tests confirmed that 'a male' in Jefferson's line was indeed the father of at least one of Sally's children. Other possible fathers had long been ruled out or disregarded due to a lack of reliable evidence. Careful examination of the birth dates of Hemings' children and Jefferson's documented travels puts him 'with' Sally during each time of conception. That does not prove anything, as he was her employer and they worked together.

Was Thomas Jefferson, a principal author of the Declaration of Independence, victim of a hate-filled opponent or was he really having sex with his personal slave? Perhaps we will never know for sure, but professors Annette Gordon-Reed and Fawn Brodie are amongst many who have revisited and re-examined the evidence in recent years, judging its reliability, accuracy and bias. Nobody knows for sure where Sally Hemings is buried. The story of the Hemings-Jefferson scandal was brought to life in the television mini-series *Sally Hemings: An American Scandal*, made in 2000, starring Sam Neill and Carmen Ejogo. It described a complicated thirty-eight-year relationship set across many countries, with Sally working for Jefferson in Paris at one point.

In 2000, more specialist scholars re-examined the paternity question and said that the Jefferson-Hemings allegation is still not proven. Previously, most historians dismissed the idea that Jefferson and Hemings had children together, although in recent times more of them are looking at the evidence and agreeing that it was probably true. In 2010, John Works, an eighth generation descendant of Thomas Jefferson's, wrote the article 'The Jefferson-Hemings Controversy: A New, Critical Look'. In this article, in an American history magazine called *Drumbeat*, the author calls for a more careful inquiry into conclusions made after the 1998 DNA testing. Works says, 'While we may never know who fathered Eston Hemings, or any of Sally Hemings' other children, we do this great man in American history a big disservice by prematurely concluding that this centuries-old paternity case has been adequately and responsibly resolved.'

McCarthyism, the Red Scare, witch-hunt trials and the senator

In the aftermath of the Second World War, the United States of America was in a very tense political state. Anti-communist feelings were running high and the nation was obsessed with beating communism. Twentieth-century Red Scares have included the latter part of the Great War (1914-18) and the years immediately following, the Russian Revolution, with the Bolsheviks' execution of Nicholas II, and the political witch-hunt that took place in America from 1947-1957 that became known as 'McCarthyism'. Nicholas II was Russia's last tsar and was in power until the country's radical upheaval. In addition, there was the post-Second World War spread of communism – Korea and China, for example and an increase in Soviet espionage. The race for atomic weapons and the start of the Cold War ushered in a new era of political friction.

There was a fear of communism spreading across the world to America. There was a degree of social agitation in the United States. Newspapers exaggerated the threat and many were scared that the Bolshevik Revolution was coming to America. The Industrial Workers of the World (an international industrial union formed in 1905) supported a number of strikes around the time of the First World War. The press fuelled the fear that left-wing agents were trying to cause chaos, bring down the country and introduce communism. In 1919, there were a number of mail-bomb scares and actual explosions in cities, all aimed at the establishment. The 1918 Sedition Act was an attempt to protect wartime morale by punishing those who abused the United States government, constitution, flag or military. It was aimed at far-left activists and other political dissenters. However, it is argued that the Act did not really tackle any real and genuine threat. There was an over-aggressive government stance on anything foreign, left-wing or with extreme ideologies, which were seen as un-American and something that must be dealt with.

Senator Joseph McCarthy was an outspoken politician who publicly accused people of being secret communists ready to undermine the authority of the United States of America. His message came at a difficult time, when many were 'on edge' about the spread of communism. This high-profile figure was unfortunately taken seriously by many, and believed by many more. He was, in fact, a ridiculous figure of fun, and a bully. He was a useless politician, only gaining a Senate seat after the war by using lies and propaganda against his opponent. He played dirty, but could not come up with the goods himself. Those he accused of being communist spent so much time defending themselves against whatever he decided to throw at them that the spotlight was taken off McCarthy himself. He was a shallow man politically, switching parties for his own advancement. If he had spoken out at any other time in history, he would not have been taken seriously for a minute. His message, for many, seemed to come at the right time, in the right place. He built on, and fuelled, political worry, turning it into panic. Even before his life in politics, opponents claimed he had fought a dirty battle to win a position as a circuit judge.

McCarthy, looking to throw dirt around for his re-election campaign and unable to boast of any successes of his own doing, took advantage of the nation's fear of the spread of communism. In February 1950, this inadequate man stepped forward and announced that he was in possession of a list from the State Department that had 205 people on it who were, in fact, members of the American Communist Party. McCarthy displayed a list of names but never made it public. Only a few names were ever put in the public domain. In addition, there was a discrepancy in the number of names on the list. McCarthy's speech at Wheeling, West Virginia, in 1950, had been questionable and some believe that his list had been a mere stage prop. Opponents questioned if he was merely quoting names from the Lee list, a former investigation into security risks.

It was as if he had thrown a lighted match onto a political fire. The public, instantly and en masse was up in arms, generally believing every word he said without question. They were furious that there were secret communists embedded in important government decision-making positions. A mere accusation seemed good enough for many Americans. The atmosphere was one of having to prove your innocence rather than the other way round. Few were brave enough to take on Senator McCarthy. There was absolute panic within numerous government departments. These witch-hunts lasted for several years, with Joseph McCarthy accusing many innocent people.

From 1946 to 1957, McCarthy was a member of the United States Senate. However, in 1953 when he became Chair of the Senate Committee on Government Operations, he had more authority, more power, more staff to assist him and the power of subpoena. People were quite rightly scared of this lying bully's false accusations. McCarthy and McCarthy supporters failed to see that anti-communism in the United States was much bigger than any one individual. Some historians believe that McCarthy's was the biggest fight against communism at that time. But this is not true; he was a minor figure who just managed to whip up a frenzy. He took advantage of the political situation and made things worse, just to take the focus off his own political failings. He was an inadequate, sad failure, and this witch-hunt made him feel important. He had a dangerous salesmanlike quality of getting his own way. He was 90 per cent hype, playing on the emotions and fears of a nation.

Senator Joseph McCarthy took the self-styled image of protector of America, with a desire to sort out the nation's worries, announcing that McCarthyism was Americanism. He called his book *McCarthyism: The Fight for America*. In it he laid down the gauntlet and manipulated American minds by promoting his own self-importance and his so-called honesty and integrity. McCarthy said, 'I feel strongly about labeling products for what they are ... truth should be labeled as truth; lies should be labeled as lies.' This was a direct attack on hidden communism. It may have also referred to homosexuals – another target of McCarthy.

Back in Britain, even *The Times* came out in support of the senator, claiming his fears were real and that his message was so serious it should affect policy-making in the West. He had other supporters in the media as well, including the influential radio announcer Fulton Lewis Jnr, who said that McCarthyism *is* Americanism. The senator accused his administration of being weak and cowardly and of having an immoral foreign policy. He accused the government of having a 'retreat and surrender' attitude to communism. Some saw him as a fascist though; an opportunist and untrustworthy. Not everybody fell for his sales patter!

The senator was a clever man and he had planted the seeds of doubt over communism very early on in his career. As early as 1946, he had been heard making Red-baiting remarks in relation to labour disagreements and in 1947 he called a New York housing estate a breeding ground for communists.

Let us also consider the point that McCarthy was successful in creating political panic because of communist growth already happening around him, and preceding him. There was already deep worry about Soviet espionage and spying rings, with a haemorrhage of secrets flooding towards the Russians. This was enough to create a Red Scare on its own, with or without McCarthyism. To prove this we need to see how serious some of those events really were. For example, in 1945, more than a thousand, stolen, classified government documents were found in offices of the left-wing magazine *Amerasia*. In 1946, a spy ring was discovered in Canada, from where atomic secrets had been sent to the Soviet Union. In 1949, Judith Coplon, an employee of the Justice Department, was convicted of passing secrets to the Soviets, although her conviction was overturned on appeal. In 1950, British physicist Dr Klaus

Fuchs, who had worked in the United States, was found giving atomic secrets to the Soviets, which led to the executions of two US Soviet spies, Julius and Ethel Rosenberg. They were convicted of selling secrets to Soviets during the Second World War and executed in 1953. There were eight years between the documents found in the offices of *Amerasia* and McCarthy becoming Chair of the Senate Committee on Government Operations. This goes some way to showing how the senator was a sideshow to what was really happening. He was there to play on fears, to feed his own desires of megalomania.

The conclusion here is that McCarthyism had limited importance in America's anti-communist fears in comparison with these great events. The American people were already concerned with world communism, events in Russia, Korea and China, and then the spying of the 1940s and 1950s. One could argue that there had also been a change in public opinion towards caution and concern, with a change in direction from the Truman administration. Americans were quite capable of having their own Red Scares without the likes of McCarthy; he was not even around politically during the first one.

The Hatch Act of 1939, which prevented Communist Party members from federal employment, showed that there were serious concerns over the issue even before McCarthy started shaking his fists. One of the peaks of anti-communist fear in the United States was the Cuban Missile Crisis of 1962. This occurred five years after McCarthy had died. The other side of the argument is that McCarthy picked up on these early events and discovered how serious they were in reality, in the actual strands of the United States government. Harold Lord Varney, for example, a supporter of McCarthyism, pointed out how almost everyone accused of being a communist by the senator on the list he read out on February 1950 was either sacked or had resigned from the State Department.

McCarthy simply added to America's reds-under-the-bed hysteria and it had snowballed from there. There were some people who asked about proof, but they were in the minority at first. The reality was that most people were terrified of their reputation being ruined. Part of Truman's UN delegation was one of McCarthy's many targets. The senator told the committee that diplomat Philip C. Jessup had an unusual affinity for communist causes. Jessup was actually cleared of the accusations, but his reputation was damaged and his career was over. He told the hearing that McCarthy did not have any proof, but the senator dragged name after name through the public dirt, accusing them of being communists, without a shred of evidence.

In support of McCarthy, Harold Lord Varney has written about hundreds of reputed security risks being examined in the preliminary hearings, without injury to reputation, with the innocent being weeded out early on. Varney said that only Fifth Amendment cases or those guilty or unfit were put under the public spotlight. This is perhaps an overgenerous analysis of the situation. Many innocent people, never convicted of any offence, lost their jobs in the State Department.

The year 1953 was the beginning of the end for Senator Joseph McCarthy as he started to investigate 'communist infiltration into the US military'. By this time people had begun to see through him and were questioning his motives and tactics. Finally, people were asking about proof! By this time he had upset many people; even President Dwight D. Eisenhower realised that McCarthy had gone too far and had to be stopped. The army decided it wasn't going to let the senator walk all over its good name. The army (as you would expect) fought back. It fired back at the accusations, stating that McCarthy had abused congressional privileges. They accused him of trying to get favours for his friend in the forces, Private Gerard David Schine. McCarthy was on the back foot and had a taste of his own medicine.

The army hearings saw Senator McCarthy take his communist accusations to a new level by 1954, when he dramatically accused the army of being 'full' of communists. McCarthy's defence was to attack and he ended up looking ridiculous. This time, he had bitten off more than he could chew. He accused the army's legal counsel's assistant, Fred Fisher, of being a communist. This was the last straw and the end of the senator. Counsel Joseph Welch defended Fred Fisher in the well-known line, 'Senator, may we not drop this? Let us not assassinate this lad further, Senator. You've done enough. Have you no sense of decency, Sir?' It is interesting to note the audience reactions and concentration in the footage of this on American Rhetoric Movie Speeches, via YouTube. The unwitting testimony shows a bored, frustrated and annoyed audience. It seems they had finally grown tired of these ridiculous allegations.

Meanwhile, articles appeared in American newspapers attacking McCarthy and his terrible methods of seeking out so-called communists. During the televised trials, the American people slowly began to realise that McCarthy had duped them. The tide of public opinion, and therefore political support, started to desert him. McCarthy had been in the right political place at the right time to make his accusations, against an international political backdrop. For a while, he got the press on his side. In his journal *Media Manipulation, Partisan Politics, or Institutional Complicity*, Michael Wreszin argues that McCarthy was able to outwit seasoned journalists with multiple untruths. His world came crashing down around him, and not before time. Things went from bad to worse for the senator from December 1954, when a censure motion was issued against him. He had now been deserted by the public, the politicians, the president and the media. McCarthy was deservedly a finished man. He drank himself to death within three years. We can argue that the relatively new medium of television had played a major role in the popularisation of McCarthy, and then his downfall at the army hearings.

There had been several anti-communist investigations or Red Scare committees in the years prior to the McCarthy witch-hunts, including the Overman Committee in 1918, which investigated German and Bolshevik elements in the United States, and the Fish Committee of 1930, which investigated communist activities in the United States. In addition, the 1950 McCarran Act (Internal Security Act) made all communists register with the Attorney General. All of this was under way long before the McCarthy hysteria. Caution against communism was already a way of life.

Throughout these years, McCarthy did have his supporters, even right up to the end, when most had deserted him. Ann Coulter, author of *Treason* (2005), claimed the senator was right and that the American government at the time was infiltrated with spies. She links her claims to the contents of the Venona project, analysis of Soviet intelligence agency messages, declassified in 1995. McCarthy's modern-day supporters state on their website that not one person who was supposedly falsely accused of being a communist by the senator ever proved otherwise. The debate continues today about whether he was right or wrong and whether or not he had any proof. There is even a website dedicated to the story, with ongoing discussion, at senatormccarthy. com. Whether or not he had any evidence, or whatever the truth really was at the time, Senator Joseph McCarthy's biggest significance was to add to, and make far worse, a sense of public paranoia about reds-under-the-bed and a possible takeover by communists, resulting in a loss of their way of life.

This second Red Scare, from approximately 1945-57, was about concern of communists directly infiltrating the United States government. It coincided with the increased fear of communist spying, the founding of the People's Republic of China, the Korean War, the Iron Curtain and the Berlin Blockade. In Canada, several Soviet spy documents were uncovered, which all added to the Red Scare. Meanwhile, at the House of Un-American Activities Committee, former communist spies claimed that communist sympathisers had already penetrated the United States government. The second Red Scare carried themes of communism taking America by invasion, subversion, destruction and infiltration. It put many on high alert because they could see what was happening around the rest of the world. It scared many people, and made others paranoid.

The congressman and the stripper

This was an interesting combination in the early 1970s that effectively ended the successful career of one of America's most powerful congressmen.

Despite the curriculum vitae of Wilbur Mills boasting of him being county judge in Arkansas, congressman 1939-77, and of a 1972 unsuccessful bid for the presidency, he will be best remembered by some as the politician caught with a stripper. For many, the memory of this incident will also overshadow his relentless efforts for cheaper health care for the most vulnerable.

In the early hours of the morning of 9 October 1974, police approached a car in Washington, DC just because it had not turned on its lights properly. This small, routine incident opened up what can be described as one of Washington's juiciest scandals. Officers found Arkansas Democrat Wilbur D. Mills, although not the driver, drunk in the back with another passenger, an Argentine stripper known on stage as Fanne Foxe. Mills' face was injured following a scuffle with Foxe. She left the scene in a hurry and jumped into the nearby Tidal Basin, an artificial lake, and was later taken to hospital. Details of the night's events were splashed over the front pages of the newspapers for weeks, with Mills issuing denials and 'no comments' at first. It was a huge embarrassment to Mills and his wife. People wanted to know what he was doing hanging round with this stripper. He had been photographed at various places and functions around town with her, and he was known to have frequented her place of work to watch her perform, which no doubt went down well with his wife! Foxe's real name was Annabelle Battistella. Her other working names included the Argentine Firecracker and the Tidal Basin Bombshell.

Soon afterwards, Mills sought treatment for his alcohol problem and was re-elected to Congress later that year. However, he was seen drunk again with Fanne Foxe, and in an embarrassing episode appeared intoxicated with Foxe's husband onstage in Boston at the Pilgrim Theater, where Foxe was dancing.

Mills did not run for re-election in 1976, perhaps seeing how difficult a re-election campaign would have been after the scandal. As chairman of the House Ways and Means Committee he had been influential over policies affecting taxation, social security and welfare, plus many others. He had served his country well for decades and was once seen as one of the most powerful members of Congress. His ongoing public relationship with Foxe was not conducive to a successful family life and political career.

Mills died on 2 May 1992 at home in Kensett, and remained very popular with the people of Arkansas. His memory lives on in the many places and institutions that have been named after him. They include the following:

- The Wilbur D. Mills Treatment Center in Searcy, Arkansas, which offers a detoxification/residential treatment programme to those with chemical addiction

- The Wilbur D. Mills University Studies High School in Sweet Home
- The Wilbur D. Mills Social Sciences Building at Hendrix College
- The Wilbur D. Mills Freeway
- The Wilbur D. Mills Lock and Dam on the Arkansas River
- Mills Park Road, Bryant, Arkansas
- Mills Street, Walnut Ridge, Arkansas

Statues of Mills can be seen at:

- Arkansas State Capitol
- Hendrix College
- Boswell Law Office, Bryant, Arkansas

President Warren Harding and the Teapot Dome scandal

Warren G. Harding (b.1865 d.1923) was the twenty-ninth president of the United States, in office from 1921-23. He was an influential, self-made newspaper publisher, a republican and a former senator. His post-First World War presidential campaign was based on promising a return to normality, with a strong economy as a major goal. His message was well received by the American people and he was victorious at the polls. His election victory was followed by appointments of friends and political contributors to a number of favourable, influential, well-paid positions within the new American government.

Harding's administration, however, was rocked by a number of scandals. The biggest one was called the Teapot Dome scandal, which was all about bribery, corruption and oil money influencing national politics of the day. This happened in Harding's cabinet, on Harding's watch and, of course, right under Harding's nose. Secretary of the Interior (and former senator) Albert B. Fall was a close friend of the Hardings. The scandal was based around several oil leases being awarded to companies, but without open competition and tendering. There seemed to be lots of dealings and handshakes behind closed doors at the White House. The dealings were complex at best, shady and illegal at worst. On behalf of Harding's government, Fall organised the lease of several oil reserves at very low prices. For example, oilman Harry Sinclair obtained leases to drill for oil at a place called Teapot Dome in Wyoming (hence the name of the scandal). Meanwhile, Edward L. Doheny acquired leases for reserves at Elk Hills in California. Strangely, Fall was paid handsomely by these people and their companies (about $400,000), for the deals. He was lining his pockets and doing his friends a favour. The awarding of leases at low prices without competition was not technically illegal, but taking the bribe certainly was illegal.

Fall tried to keep his business secret, but the vast and sudden improvement in his finances and material wealth in general aroused suspicion. By 1924, people were still asking how Fall had become so wealthy so quickly. A two-year investigation into the oil leases had not produced anything. Suspiciously, offices were ransacked, paperwork was going missing and some were refusing to cooperate. Investigators only had a breakthrough when they found evidence of a loan from Doheny to Fall, and the scandal was wide open again. There were several court cases throughout the 1920s relating to the scandal and the Teapot Dome and Elk Hills were taken back in 1927.

Fall was convicted of bribery and sentenced to one year in prison. Doheny escaped conviction, but Sinclair was imprisoned for contempt of court. It could be argued that the Teapot Dome scandal showed President Harding's poor leadership skills, and the number of his friends that had been appointed to the Cabinet introduced corruption into everyday politics.

The Newport sex scandal

The sexual relationships between United States Navy personnel in Newport, Rhode Island, and the civilian population came under scrutiny in this 1919 scandal. The target was possible illicit homosexual contact. There had been talk of a homosexual subculture at Newport and officials ordered an investigation after several reports of homosexual shenanigans. The investigation was authorised by a young assistant secretary of the navy, Roosevelt – future president, Franklin D. Roosevelt.

Undercover enlisted personnel were sent out to effectively spy on suspected homosexual behaviour. During the investigation many sailors were arrested and appeared before a military tribunal. After three weeks, seventeen sailors were charged with sodomy and scandalous behaviour. It was mainly local church leaders who complained to the White House over how the case was handled, with some people locked up for weeks without being charged, and vicious, deleterious and underhand dealings with suspects. It named and shamed Secretary of the Navy Josephus Daniels and Roosevelt. In July 1920, while investigations continued, Roosevelt left his post of assistant secretary of the navy, accepting the Democratic Party's nomination for vice-president.

In July 1921, the *New York Times* highlighted the anger at the initial investigation using navy personnel to catch other navy personnel. The headline read: 'Charges of Immorally Employing Men Do Officials Injustice'.

In the same month, a subcommittee of the Senate Committee on Naval Affairs denounced both Daniels and Roosevelt for the methods used in the Newport investigations.

Franklin D. Roosevelt's affair

Roosevelt was the thirty-second president of the United States of America, 1933-45, winning an impressive four elections. He battled polio and spent much of his time in a wheelchair, and had great difficulty in standing or walking. Out of the thousands of photographs of Roosevelt, there are only four of him in a wheelchair. He would always hide his disability by leaning on something or someone while a photo was being taken. He had an agreement with the press for them to not talk about his disability.

However, it was his sham marriage and his affair that was a scandal. He had an eye for the ladies and when he was secretary of the navy during the First World War he began an affair with his wife's social secretary. It was a relationship that was to last for years and that would effectively end his marriage, certainly from the waist down. Playing so close to home, he was soon found out and his wife Eleanor decided to stick by her husband on the condition that he ended his relationship with the woman. He promised to do so, but had no intention of keeping his word. By 1932, a fed-up Eleanor decided to take a lover herself. Her husband was not impressed because there was an election coming up and any scandal might jeopardise his chances of winning.

Eleanor eventually took a female companion, rather more of a scandal back then than it would be today, perhaps. But she became intimate with a reporter called Lorena Hickok. During the Second World War, Franklin Roosevelt and his lover lived in one wing of the White House and Eleanor Roosevelt and her lover lived in another wing. They remained completely separate. The president got away with all this because many regarded him as a hero during the Great Depression and the Second World War.

When Franklin D. Roosevelt was dying he spent his final moments with his mistress. His wife was many miles away at the time. Roosevelt died on 12 April 1945, without Eleanor being able to say goodbye. His mistress quietly slipped away from their Warm Springs retreat, in Georgia, before the news broke to the rest of the country. When Eleanor arrived late that night, she learned that her husband's mistress had been there before her.

President John F. Kennedy – did he like it hot?

Conspiracy theories can have the 'wow' factor and make us question what really happened. Usually it is just mischief-makers and their overactive mouths. Whether it is Elvis working in a chip shop in Yorkshire, the Princess of Wales being murdered by spies or the 1969 landing on the Moon being faked in a television studio, it sets tongues wagging and historians wondering.

Some Like It Hot actress Marilyn Monroe was rumoured to be having an affair with the then US President John F. Kennedy. By the time she had seductively sung 'Happy Birthday Mr President' in May 1962 for his birthday, the scandal machine was in full throttle. Many thought she was also sleeping with the president's brother, Attorney General Robert Kennedy, as well! This was political scandal at its best and it was about to get really interesting: John F. Kennedy supposedly ended the relationship because Monroe had been planning to spill the beans. The actress suddenly died in mysterious circumstances. In August 1962, she was found lying naked on her bed in her Brentwood home in California, next to an empty bottle of sleeping pills. The coroner at the time described it as a 'possible suicide'. There has never been a more definitive answer to Marilyn's death than that. Perhaps the uncertainty has helped fuel the scandal.

John F. Kennedy had used Marilyn, had his wicked way and discarded her soon afterwards, apparently telling her she would never be First Lady material. Monroe had fallen for him and her feelings had grown. By the time she died she was dependent on prescription drugs and alcohol and had often been in a precarious emotional state, fearful of rejection. Being rejected by Kennedy, and the president getting his brother to tell Monroe it was over, was probably enough to push her over the edge. To John F. Kennedy, their liaison had been a brief fling; to her, it had been more. This was one of the most beautiful women in the world and certainly not used to male rejection.

Questions still remain about who administered the drugs; was it her, or someone else? Was it an accident or was it deliberate? Some suggest that because she had been in a precarious mental state, suicide was indeed possible. Others suggest a more sinister path. Over the decades there have been many theories and the finger has been pointed at various people, including murder by federal agents, JFK's brother Robert, fascists and even the Mob. Marilyn Monroe had appeared in thirty films, including *The Prince and the Showgirl*, *The Seven-Year Itch* and *Some Like It Hot*, and fans demanded to know how and why she had gone. Had JFK arranged for her to be silenced to protect his reputation? The affair was scandal enough at the time, but murder? Surely not.

The scandal of the forgotten soldiers in Vietnam – or is it just a conspiracy theory?

America and Vietnam were engaged in ground warfare from 1965 to 1973, and in the end the Americans withdrew their troops from an 'unwinnable war'. But did the US government leave behind some of its own men? Some believe that 'Missing in Action' or 'Killed in Action' personnel might have been written off too early. In polls during the 1980s, more than 70 per cent of American citizens said they thought a number of troops could still be there. Consider the fact that the Vietnamese defeated the French in 1954, and in 1976 the last French prisoner was released by Vietnam. Any American military personnel listed as 'missing' or 'prisoner' were declared 'dead' in 1978 by the Carter administration. Questions were asked about men who had been taken as prisoners to Laos, Cambodia and Russia. More questions were asked about the Vietnamese incomplete prisoner lists. In 1981, the Vietnamese asked the Reagan administration for money in return for prisoners.

Some people insist that the war has long been over and stories of forgotten prisoners are just conspiracy theories. However, Robert Garwood, former United States Marine Corps private, was captured and taken prisoner in 1965 but did not return home to the US until 1979. He claimed he had been held prisoner and had seen other prisoners. The US government accused him of collaborating with the enemy, he was discharged and forced to forfeit his entire army back pay. Garwood denied the charges of collaboration and in turn accused America's Department of Defense of rewriting history. In 1992, a US task force visited the sites where Garwood said he had seen live US prisoners but found no evidence of them. Films like *Rambo* and *Missing in Action* either served to fuel the conspiracy theories or made a case for prisoners still being held in Vietnam.

Meanwhile, critics of the Americans point out that the country dropped millions of tons of chemicals on the Vietnamese people, troops and crops. Recent reports suggest that, four decades later, the health of hundreds of thousands of Vietnamese is still affected by the use of chemicals such as the herbicide Agent Orange. At the same time, returning US troops also complained of poor health because of the chemical weapons. Yet thirty years later, America was telling the world how wrong Iraq was to have chemical weapons.

Finally, it would be an endless task to discuss scandals and stories from wars throughout history, but on the subject of the Vietnam War, another scandal should be mentioned. It was an attack that shamed many Americans. It was called the My Lai Massacre, and took place on 16 March 1968. It was probably one of the most infamous events of the conflict.

Just after dawn on this day, the village of 700 inhabitants was attacked by three platoons of US troops from C Company. Second Lieutenant William Calley was ordered to take his men to My Lai village as part of a search and destroy mission. They had been told of enemy activity in the area. Troops from 1 Platoon opened fire on the villagers, mainly women and children. One witness said a US soldier executed two 5-year-old boys. The villagers had been mutilated, had their throats cut and been shot. There was nobody of fighting age or ability, as the men were all out working in the fields. The US troops faced no opposition from the terrified villagers. When the men returned they took three days to bury the dead.

Nobody is sure of exactly how many were murdered and executed by the American troops. Figures range from 175 to 504. The American government admitted 347 killings during its investigation into the brutality.

Several soldiers were charged and acquitted over the massacre. It was only William Calley that was punished, with life in prison with hard labour. He was released after little more than three years and had hundreds of thousands of supporters who agreed with his plea that he had been following orders. Supporters said that US troops were aware that any Vietnamese, regardless of gender or age, could have been an enemy sympathiser, assisting with attacks on American troops.

The Watergate scandal

Watergate was certainly America's top scandal – even, perhaps, beyond its own borders. It resulted in the resignation of President Nixon in August 1974. It began in June 1972, after five men were arrested in Washington for breaking into the headquarters of the Democratic National Committee at the Watergate Complex, which is where the name of the scandal comes from. A link was proven between those who broke in and the Committee for the Re-election of The President. By the end of the entire Watergate investigation, forty-three other people were put on trial, including several senior Nixon officials. Nobody has ever been completely sure about the original purpose of the break-in. It has never really been established.

From the beginning President Nixon tried to cover up any connection between the Watergate burglary and the White House. An investigation suggested that events surrounding Watergate were just a few of a number of questionable activities ordered by the White House at the time. It was then revealed that Nixon had recorded all his personal phone calls in the Oval Office since 1971. In February 1973, a US Senate committee demanded Nixon hand over the tapes, but he refused. The case went all the way to the

Supreme Court, in United States vs Richard M. Nixon. He lost the case and the tapes were handed over. They provided proof that he had been involved in obstructing the Watergate investigation. Recordings showed Nixon had clearly tried to cover up the break-in.

The connection between the break-in and the re-election committee was shown by the country's media coverage at the time, especially in *The Washington Post* and *The New York Times*. The two journalists behind most of the revelations won awards for their work. Bob Woodward and Carl Bernstein uncovered information suggesting knowledge of the corruption went as far as the Justice Department, the FBI, the CIA, and even the White House. Chief among the *Post's* anonymous sources was an individual whom Woodward and Bernstein had nicknamed Deep Throat.

In March 1974, a grand jury in Washington, DC indicted several former aides of President Nixon, who became known as the 'Watergate Seven' for conspiring to hinder the Watergate investigation. With the impeachment procedure already in place and Nixon quickly losing political support, he decided to resign rather than risk being removed from office. He quit in August 1974. The American public, who already felt deceived about what was happening in the Vietnam War, continued to lose faith in the White House. Public confidence in Nixon and in the government as a whole had been eroded.

Nixon's resignation speech to the nation soon followed, and included the following excerpts:

In all the decisions I have made in my public life, I have always tried to do what was best for the Nation. Throughout the long and difficult period of Watergate, I have felt it was my duty to persevere, to make every possible effort to complete the term of office to which you elected me. In the past few days, however, it has become evident to me that I no longer have a strong enough political base in the Congress to justify continuing that effort.

I would have preferred to carry through to the finish whatever the personal agony it would have involved, and my family unanimously urged me to do so. But the interest of the Nation must always come before any personal considerations.

I have never been a quitter. To leave office before my term is completed is abhorrent to every instinct in my body. But as President, I must put the interest of America first ... therefore, I shall resign the Presidency effective at noon tomorrow. Vice-President Ford will be sworn in as President at that hour in this office.

As a result of the resignation Congress immediately dropped its impeachment proceedings against Nixon. He was then succeeded by Vice-President Gerald Ford, who in September 1974 granted a full and unconditional pardon to Nixon. This also gave him immunity from any future prosecution in relation to Watergate and his time in office.

Chris Lee smiles for the camera!

A Republican member of the United States House of Representatives, Chris Lee ended his political career in a flash after an exchange of emails. The congressman entered into correspondence with a woman in Maryland whom he met on the online forum craigslist.com and also sent a topless photo of himself to her.

The correspondence was said to be rather charming and pleasant. However, Lee told the 34-year-old woman that he was a lobbyist, divorced, aged thirty-

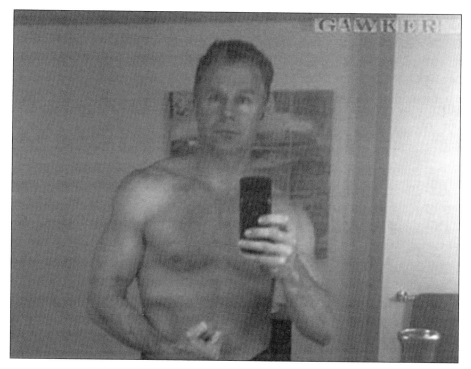

Chris Lee and the photo he took of himself that ended his political career. (Reproduced by kind permission of gawker.com)

nine, *and* he used his real name. When the woman Googled him, she found that he was a married congressman. She handed over the email correspondence to a news blog and it went public. There followed a flurry of Tweets and emails around Washington and events moved on very quickly.

Lee resigned as soon as the story went public and issued a statement apologising to his family. It said, 'I regret the harm that my actions have caused my family, my staff and my constituents … I deeply and sincerely apologise to them all. I have made profound mistakes and I promise to work as hard as I can to seek their forgiveness.'

His fall from grace happened within hours, as *The Washington Post* described it, 'undone at the speed of the digital age.' This makes it one of the quickest, short-lived scandals on Capitol Hill. His swift response to the scandal was a defence mechanism to make it go away. Chris Lee had served from January 2009 until his sudden resignation in February 2011.

Bill Clinton and Monica Lewinsky

In 1998, there was a White House scandal that almost brought down an American presidency. It was the biggest scandal in Washington since Watergate brought down Nixon in the 1970s, and the press could smell its enormity. It was the affair between President Bill Clinton and the intern Monica Lewinsky.

The story had been around for some time and it was only a case of when it would hit the headlines. It started with internet gossip, which reported that a well-known magazine had pulled a story about Clinton's alleged sexual relationship with a former intern. However, when it did break it was not a major newspaper, breakfast television, rolling news story, or anything like that. It was the online news aggregation *Drudge Report* that started it off. A *Newsweek* journalist had been anxious to break allegations of a Clinton/ Lewinsky affair for a year but had been pulled at the last moment by nervous editors. *Drudge* did run it though, some three days before the mainstream press – the equivalent of years in the world of journalism! Almost overnight, Monica Lewinsky became the most famous woman in the world. Every TV and radio station, magazine, newspaper and website was running this story in one form or another.

The Clinton/Lewinsky scandal had actually begun after the Clinton/ Jones scandal. On 6 May 1994, Paula Jones filed a sexual harassment suit against Clinton. She claimed that he had exposed himself to her in 1991 when he was Arkansas state governor. At this time she was a lowly state employee, well below Clinton's status. There had been a deal struck to settle out of

The White House – scene of the scandal. (Phil Seaman)

court but the sticking point was over an apology. Clinton had to say sorry, and he refused to do that. Clinton paid $850,000 to Paula Jones but he did not apologise to her. Neither did he admit that he had done anything wrong. Bill Clinton always insisted on his innocence in the Paula Jones case and was never found guilty of any offence by a court. However, lawyers had been looking for other women who had worked in government and who may have been sexually involved with Clinton. They were trying to establish some kind of pattern in his behaviour. It was during this investigation that the Clinton/Lewinsky affair was uncovered.

In summer 1996, Lewinsky had told fellow Pentagon employee Linda Tripp of her alleged relationship and Tripp had made a tape recording of their conversations. In December 1997, Lewinsky was subpoenaed by lawyers for Paula Jones and filed an affidavit in the Jones case, denying she had ever had a sexual relationship with President Clinton. A few days later, Tripp sent the tapes to her lawyer. More and more people were in the loop about Lewinsky and Clinton. In his deposition in the Paula Jones case, in January 1998 Clinton denied having a sexual relationship with Lewinsky. Within days, it was all the press was interested in and the scandal erupted. Clinton again denied his affair with Lewinsky and said he never asked her to lie about it in court. Soon after, Clinton came out with the famous line: 'I did not have sexual relations with that woman, Miss Lewinsky.' There had been many exchanges of gifts between the two, and several sexual encounters including a famous one that involved a cigar!

An investigation was already under way and a grand jury hearing was to follow. Clinton had to answer questions set against him, and a number of allegations were made about his sexual behaviour. On 10 March 1998, Kathleen Willey, a former White House volunteer, accused the president of fondling her and testified before the grand jury. By July 1998, Lewinsky was trying to get an 'immunity from prosecution' agreement. She admitted that she had had a sexual relationship with President Clinton but refused to say that Clinton told her to lie about it. As part of the deal she gave prosecutors a dark blue dress that she alleged may have contained physical evidence of a sexual relationship. In August 1998, President Bill Clinton became the first sitting president to testify before a grand jury investigating his own conduct. At this point he went on national television and admitted that he had indeed had an inappropriate relationship with Monica Lewinsky. He told the American people that he took full responsibility for his actions. He said: 'I did have a relationship with Miss Lewinsky that was not appropriate.' He said he had not admitted the affair earlier because he had been embarrassed and also said he had not asked anyone to lie about the relationship for him.

In the following month more than four hours of Clinton's videotaped grand jury testimony was aired by the networks. Soon afterwards, the House Judiciary Committee said it would consider a resolution to begin an impeachment inquiry against the president in early October. It had been a rollercoaster of events that had all started over questions relating to land purchases and accusations of sexual misconduct from several women, culminating in the Lewinsky affair and the question of whether or not the president had lied under oath. Clinton was charged with perjury and later, Articles of Impeachment were brought against him. He could have been looking at the end of his political career. A twenty-one-day trial followed and the president was acquitted of all charges. He was impeached and eventually found not guilty of high crimes and misdemeanours in a senate trial, and remained in office as president.

The sex offender mayor

In 2003, the former Mayor of Waterbury, Connecticut, USA, Philip Giordano, was convicted of fourteen counts of using an interstate device (his mobile phone) to arrange sexual contact with children. He was arrested in 2001 after he arranged for a prostitute to bring along her niece and daughter. One of the girls was eight years old and the other was just ten. Giordano was also convicted of violating the girls' human rights. The former Republican mayor had been a successful politician until then, winning three mayoral elections although failing in his bid to get elected to the US Senate.

On sentencing him to thirty-seven years behind bars, US District Judge Alan Nevas told him, 'Your conduct is the worst I have ever seen. I've seen drug dealers, murderers. What you did is indescribable.' Giordano claimed his innocence and said that he had not done anything criminal. The judge said exactly what he thought about the man before him, calling him a sexual predator and accusing him of preying on the young girls and destroying their innocence for his own sexual desire.

Months earlier, Giordano had promised to get tough on crime, yet he could have faced a life sentence under federal guidelines for his own crimes. However, the judge gave him a lesser sentence because he had cooperated on a recent federal investigation of a political corruption case. He is currently serving his sentence at the United States Penitentiary, Marion, a high-security federal prison based in Illinois, and is due for release in 2033.

Sex club allegations

Republican Jack Ryan dropped out of the Illinois senatorial race in 2004 after allegations against him emerged from previous divorce proceedings. In the confidential divorce papers his former wife Jeri Ryan alleged that Jack wanted her to have sex with him in sex clubs in New York, New Orleans and Paris while other people looked on. Jack Ryan denied all the allegations and indicated that it would be discussed too much in the campaign if he stayed in the race. He said it would simply turn off voters and so he decided to pull out. Meanwhile, Jeri Ryan, a former TV actress who had appeared in *Star Trek*, denied anything happened on these trips.

Other state politicians and campaigners insisted that the former businessman and teacher was not forced to pull out but that he had very little support, if any, from others. The confidential divorce papers had been sealed by a court in California several years previously. However, certain media outlets pressed for the opening of the documents when he was in the race for the Senate.

Jack Ryan called this the first 'sexless sex scandal' because there was no sex and the person involved was his wife anyway! He also claimed that his former wife and he had opposed a judge's decision to release the sealed information from the divorce papers. He said that the judge decided the public's right to know seemed more important to the court than the effect it might have on the Ryans' 9-year-old son.

Speaking on the US cable news and information channel MSNBC, Jack Ryan said that there were other things more important to him than the race for the Senate, such as a good relationship with his son. Remaining professional and dignified, he refused to attack his ex-wife, saying that she was a good woman and a good mother. Jeri Ryan also later issued a statement saying that Jack was a good man and to her knowledge had never been unfaithful to her.

Utah congresswoman caught on camera

In 2004 the estranged husband of Utah congresswoman Katherine Bryson put up a hidden surveillance camera in the apartment she owned but was renting to her son. The husband, Kay Bryson, Utah County Attorney, said he put it up to try to catch a burglar. They were going through a bitter divorce at the time and the camera recorded Katherine with her lover. She notified Salt Lake City Police, claiming that because her estranged husband had used the technical services of county employees to install the cameras, it was technically an abuse of power. She accused him of invasion of privacy, alleging that his sole intention was to spy on her rather than catch a burglar. A police investigation disagreed and Kay was cleared of any wrongdoing.

The Washington, DC madam and her saucy little book

Deborah Jeane Palfrey was a well-known Washington, DC madam who provided top-class escorts to the city's gents between 1993 and 2006. She had served time in 1992 for pimping. Meanwhile, her agency was a legal, top-class, erotic service. Hundreds of well-placed, successful men got very twitchy when word got out that she had kept on paper records of all phone calls, and that those detailed records weighed 50lbs – that is a lot of paper! The records had the capability of shaming 10,000 clients. There were resignations and seats lost at elections because of this woman.

Palfrey was arrested in 2006, had $1.5 million of assets frozen and was charged in connection with money laundering and federal racketeering. In April 2008 she was convicted on all counts but was found hanged before she could start her sentence. She had been barred from selling her phone lists so had put the whole lot up on her website, creating panic in political circles. Palfrey had also instructed her lawyers to investigate if she should be found dead and the authorities claimed 'suicide', and the lawyers sued Florida Police Department for all its files on their client.

Toilet encounters with a United States senator

On 11 June 2007, United States Republican Senator Larry Craig was at the centre of a police investigation into alleged lewd conduct in an airport men's room. The Idaho senator was arrested after an undercover police officer alleged that Craig had signalled him in the toilet stall next door at Minneapolis-St Paul International Airport.

Craig had tapped his right foot and used it to touch the left foot of the officer, and then waved his hand beneath the stall partition. Police Sergeant Dave Karsnia wrote in his report that the signals he witnessed suggested that Larry Craig wanted to engage in lewd conduct. The senator said that the officer simply misinterpreted his actions.

After he was taken in for questioning the senator produced his business card to identify himself and said, 'What do you think of that?' The police officer seemed unimpressed and went ahead with his questioning and investigation as normal. Senators who discussed the matter later were said to be more especially worried about the business card allegation.

On 8 August Craig entered a guilty plea to a lesser charge of disorderly conduct. However, he said that his pleading guilty was an overreaction. Later, in a press conference, he asserted his innocence. He always denied being gay. He was fined just over $500 for the incident.

*Minneapolis-St
Paul International
Airport – scene
of the incident.*
(Verity & Aaron
Bhyre)

Three of the best, US-style – three quick-round scandal stories

Texan Democrat John Young

John Young (b.1916 d.2002) served in the United States House of Representatives between 1957 and 1979, and was a former lawyer and judge, and had also served in the US Navy. His successful career came under the spotlight in a rather unpleasant sex allegation case. In 1976, a former female member of his staff accused Young of asking for sex in return for her keeping her job. Young was a married man and had five children. Sadly, his wife took her own life in 1977 by shooting herself. The following year he was defeated in the election and left office in 1979.

Mississippi Republican Jon Hinson

In 1978, Jon Hinson (b.1942 d.1995) was a political aide to Republican Thad Cochran, who did not seek re-election but instead successfully ran for the Senate. Hinson, in turn, succeeded him but in 1980 he admitted that four years earlier, while working as an aide, he had been arrested by police for committing an obscene act. He had exposed himself to an undercover policeman. He refused to resign, blamed it on the drink, denied he was gay and was re-elected. In 1981 he was arrested for his sexual conduct with a male employee at the Library of Congress, resigned and later admitted he was gay. He died at the age of fifty-three after breathing failure, which was a result of Aids.

Aaron Burr

Aaron Burr (b.1756 d.1836) was the third vice-president serving under President Thomas Jefferson, and was previously an attorney general and a soldier. During what became known as the Burr Conspiracy of 1804-07, he tried to snatch a large piece of land in the Louisiana Purchase. The area had changed ownership several times. Burr's aim was to actually set up his own country. He was arrested for treason but the charges were dropped. Another Burr scandal centred on his fatal duel with a political rival called Alexander Hamilton. Burr killed Hamilton but charges were eventually dropped.

* * *

The politician, the affair, the love child and the booze

This sounds like a lethal cocktail of scandal … and it is! Former Republican congressman from Staten Island, Vito Fossella, was caught drink-driving in 2008. The married father of three told police he was rushing to see his sick daughter. He gave the address of Laura Fay, a former US Air Force lieutenant colonel. The press began to dig deep and Fossella issued a statement detailing his drunk driving charge, also admitting an extramarital affair with Laura Fay and announcing that their daughter was three years old. His 'other family' lived nearby. When the scandal broke he admitted his errors, said there were some deep wounds to heal and did not seek re-election. He pointed out the need to move on with his life.

Eliot Spitzer – the governor and the hookers

Eliot Spitzer was the New York governor who resigned in March 2008 after authorities claimed he had spent thousands of dollars to arrange meetings with prostitutes over several months. Federal agents had him under surveillance in 2008. Spitzer met call girl Kristen in a hotel in Washington, booking in under a friend's name.

He was investigated after his bank reported a number of suspicious money transactions. Rules that allow banks to raise this alarm were created for them to help tackle terrorists or drug dealers. Spitzer's supporters claim that because he was clearly neither of these, the investigation should have gone no further. Others claim he was targeted by political enemies because he is a wealthy Democrat. It turned out that the payments were to the Emperors Club, where girls cost from $1,000 per hour and had diamond ratings on the club's website. Later, the club's madam published a book making claims about Spitzer's likes as well as details of her other clients.

The scandal, yet again, ignited the ongoing debate about whether or not prostitution should be legalised. Spitzer had no option other than to resign. His position was made untenable as he was responsible for enforcing the law. He lost everything because of his dealing with the escort club. There is no real evidence that Spitzer was specifically targeted for investigation, but the events are viewed suspiciously by some experienced former prosecutors. Thousands of emails and phone calls were intercepted while the agency was being watched. Kristen received a lot of media attention after the scandal and her MySpace page had 12,000,000 visits. She went on to pose nude for *Playboy* magazine in May 2010. In July 2013, he announced his candidacy for New York City Comptroller.

More politicians and prostitutes

In June 1976, United States Congressman Allan Howe (Utah) hit the self-destruct button and ruined his chances of re-election by soliciting two police decoy prostitutes. He did not resign, despite calls from the opposition, but lost his bid for re-election that year. He was found guilty in court in July 1976, appealed and lost. He received a thirty-day suspended sentence, plus costs. He resumed a career in law in Washington, DC. He died in December 2000.

Robert Edmund Bauman (b.1937) also kissed goodbye to his political career after being charged with attempting to solicit sex from a 16-year-old male prostitute. The former member of the US House of Representatives from Maryland's 1st congressional district was seeking re-election in 1980 when the incident happened. The charges were dropped after Bauman said he was suffering from alcoholism and completed a court-supervised programme. He was defeated in the election that December.

A Clinton political strategist resigned after a newspaper revealed he had been having an affair with a prostitute in Washington, DC. This happened in 1996 and was a huge embarrassment to those involved, especially when the woman concerned, Sherry Ann Rowlands, claimed that Dick Morris had even let her listen in to a phone call made from the president to him. He had served Bill Clinton as State Governor in Arkansas and at the White House. In his departing statement he said: 'While I served I sought to avoid the limelight because I did not want to become the message … now I resign so I will not become the issue.' However, he later turned on the Clintons, working as a political pundit and speaking negatively about them both. In 2006, as Hillary Clinton pursued the top job at the White House, Morris made his feelings very clear by saying that he would leave the country if she won.

In the spring of 1976, Nixon confidant and Louisiana Democrat Joe D. Waggoner was arrested after trying to pay for sex with an undercover policewoman. He offered the 'prostitute' $50 to have sex with him. The scandal in Washington did not kill off his career as he was re-elected in the autumn and retired in 1978.

The Mayflower Hotel

Washington, DC's historic hotel has been referred to as the city's second-best address after the White House. Since it opened in 1925 it has been patronised by senators, presidents and superstars. It became known as the 'Grande Dame of Washington, DC', with more gold trim than any other building in the United States, except for the Library of Congress.

The hotel has been at the centre of several political scandals over the years. Monica Lewinsky stayed there when her liaisons with President Clinton were in the news. It was here too that the iconic picture was taken of Lewinsky next to Clinton at a 1996 campaign event. In 2008, *The New York Times* claimed

The Mayflower Hotel – a scene of action and scandal. (Phil Seaman)

New York Governor Eliot Spitzer entertained his $1,000-an-hour call girl in room 871. President Kennedy supposedly had a mistress at the hotel, Judith Campbell Exner, who also sneaked into the White House when his wife was away.

The website historichotels.org describes the Mayflower as setting the standard for elegance and beauty. Meanwhile, the hotel has hosted every US presidential inaugural ball since that of Calvin Coolidge and has hosted events that have 'changed the course of human affairs'. It has been frequented not just by politicians, but by royalty, sportspeople, singers and film stars.

George W. Bush – you missed!

I tried to work out how I could justify putting this story in under the heading 'scandal' because it was absolutely hilarious: someone threw their shoes in protest at the then US President George W. Bush. In the end I decided to include it because I think it was a scandal that he missed! In some parts of the world it is considered an insult to even show someone the soles of your shoes.

It was an unannounced visit, in 2008, by Bush to Iraq and at a press conference he faced a small team of seated journalists alongside Iraqi Prime Minister Nouri al-Maliki as they talked about their signing of a political agreement. It was a journalist who threw the shoes in anger, shouting to Bush: 'This is a farewell gift, you dog.' Bush ducked, not once, but twice, successfully. Fellow journalists, as well as one of the White House staff members, surrounded the reporter and prevented him from doing any more damage.

Bush's security team appeared at the speed of an asthmatic snail while the two politicians stood with dignity and waited calmly. Bush later joked that all he could say was that the shoes were a size ten.

Bushisms

Meanwhile, is it a scandal that someone who said the following was ever allowed to lead a country? George W. Bush said some stupid things during his time in office – here are just a few of them:

- 'Our enemies are innovative and resourceful and so are we. They never stop thinking about new ways to harm our country and our people and neither do we.'
- 'The people in Louisiana must know that all across our country there's a lot of prayer – prayer for those whose lives have been turned upside down. And I'm one of them.'
- 'Anyone engaging in illegal financial transactions will be caught and persecuted.'
- 'This is my maiden voyage; my first speech since I was the president of the United States, and I couldn't think of a better place to give it than Calgary, Canada.'
- 'They misunderestimated me.'
- 'I've been in the Bible every day since I've been the president.'
- 'I remember meeting a mother of a child who was abducted by the North Koreans right here in the Oval Office.'
- 'Let's make sure that there is certainty during uncertain times in our economy.'
- 'I'll be long gone before some smart person ever figures out what happened inside this Oval Office.'
- 'We want people owning their home – we want people owning a business.'
- 'Removing Saddam Hussein was the right decision early in my presidency, it is the right decision now, and it will be the right decision ever.'
- 'All I can tell you is when the governor calls, I answer his phone.'

- 'If you've got a chicken factory, a chicken-plucking factory, or whatever you call them, you know what I'm talking about.'
- 'That's why we are inconveniencing air traffickers, to make sure nobody is carrying weapons on airplanes.' (Discussing the continuing need for heightened airline security.)
- 'I recently met with the finance minister of the Palestinian Authority, [and] was very impressed by his grasp of finances.'

Sarah Palin's Turkeygate

Well done, Sarah Palin, former Alaska governor and vice-presidential candidate for the worst photo opportunity of 2008 (or perhaps ever). Dubbed Wattlegate by some of the media, she pardoned a Thanksgiving turkey at a farm in Wasilla. After that she stood there and gave an interview to a reporter while dozens of other turkeys were being slaughtered just a few feet behind her. It made her look like a fool.

'I'll be in charge of the turkey,' grinned Palin when asked by the TV reporter what she was doing at Thanksgiving, as a man behind her was shoving a live turkey into a cone as it struggled and was killed. There was blood everywhere and Sarah Palin was still happy, still talking about opportunities, budgets and all manner of things. I doubt whether anybody was listening to her that much. They were probably transfixed on the little man at the back slaughtering and looking into the camera as he did the deed.

David Letterman later joked that she might be able to see Russia from Alaska, but she could not see what was happening 5 feet behind her. Nobody advised her to step a few feet to the left or a few feet to the right, which would have saved a whole lot of embarrassment.

It was not the first time that Palin made a fool of herself. As Republican vice-presidential nominee in 2008, she fell victim to Canadian pranksters. Comedian Marc-Antoine Audette called her from his Montreal radio show impersonating the French President Nicolas Sarkozy. He invited her to go hunting to kill some birds. He carried on with the prank for six minutes before owning up. By that time, everyone had had a good laugh at her expense. Once again, her adviser and staff had let her down and failed to protect her.

Another bad interview

Sarah Palin has a record of giving bad interviews. One of them was to CBS News anchor Katie Couric during her vice-president candidacy. Palin made one silly comment after another: not being able to name a newspaper she read, complaining about Putin flying over Alaskan airspace, not being able to answer some questions and only being able to name one Supreme Court decision. The United States Supreme Court is the third arm (judicial) of American government. It rules on whether legislation is within the parameters of the Constitution and is the highest court in the land.

Palin's string of silly interviews were almost as bad as Texas Governor George W. Bush not being able to name many world leaders in a TV interview in his 1999 campaign to become US president. He failed to name a number of leaders, including those in Chechnya and India.

Chapter Three

The Rest of the World

AUSTRIA

A wave of Austrian scandals

A lack of trust has become a part of everyday Austrian politics, from 2004, with a series of corruption scandals where dodgy business deals mix with smart-suited politicians and lobbyists. It has become a country synonymous with envelopes full of dirty cash being passed around. The voters and the decent politicians are fed up with how deals are done. After a wave of scandals and abuses of office, suspicion has become part of the Austrian culture. Many of the politicians spend time accusing each other and fighting over various investigations, including that of the missing billions of euros, money laundering and bribery. A number of former politicians and ministers have been at the centre of the questioning. Other scandals have included suspected embezzlement in connection with state-owned apartments, kickbacks for government contracts and misappropriation of public funds.

BULGARIA

Bulgarian blackmail

The potential for widespread scandal was revealed in Bulgaria in June 2012. We all hope that our elected officials act in our best interests but this came into question after a major prostitution ring was busted by Bulgarian police. A senior politician made some staggering claims linking organised crime and prostitution rings to the potential blackmailing of certain politicians. He claimed that mobsters had influential information on certain political officials. He would not name anyone involved but suggested that some politicians had actually been recorded with their prostitutes. He did not elaborate any further, suggesting that the information had not actually been used. At the time of writing, Bulgaria has one of the worst sex-trafficking records in the world, with many of the country's modelling agencies acting as a front for prostitution. However, Bulgaria is making real efforts to tackle its trafficking problems. A government official stated that in the transition to democracy over two decades some politicians had benefitted from the services of various groups behind organised crime, keeping inappropriate relationships with rather dubious characters.

CANADA

Sex with the secretary ends in disaster

John Brownlee was not the first man to play away from home with a young girl at work and he will not be the last, for sure. However, in 1934 Brownlee was an important and well-known Canadian politician, a provincial premier. His affair with Vivian MacMillan turned sour and finished off his career, and that of many others, too.

The John Brownlee sex scandal happened in Alberta, Canada. Eighteen-year-old MacMillan was a secretary for Brownlee's attorney general. MacMillan claimed her three-year affair with Brownlee was a result of his emotional and physical pressure and claims that she was persuaded to have sex with him partly because of Brownlee's disabled wife. Vivian MacMillan said sex was always given to Brownlee under pressure and that there was no love. She claimed to have occasionally had sex out of terror and because she was told it was her duty. Outside her 'duties' to Brownlee, she was trying to have a normal relationship.

There was a spectacular court case in 1934 before Justice William Ives, where MacMillan and her father sued for seduction. The tort of seduction was when an unmarried woman sought damages from a seducer, usually orchestrated by her father, if consent to sex occurred because of his misrepresentation. The legal basis rested on an old-fashioned view of a father's property interest in his daughter's chastity.

The trial was a huge political sex scandal and everybody was talking about it. It was a very public and very humiliating experience for Brownlee, who denied any sexual activity with the woman and said that if there had in fact been sex against her consent then he should be on trial for rape and not seduction. Being on trial for the latter, he argued, proved the MacMillans' financial motives. The jury said it found too many inconsistencies in Brownlee's defence and therefore found in favour of the plaintiffs, awarding them $15,000 between them. However, the judge intervened and overturned the decision. He was in turn overruled by an appeal court. Brownlee made the decision to resign and stepped down in July 1934.

Tunagate

Canadian Prime Minister Brian Mulroney was left with egg on his face (or should we say tuna?) in 1985 after a TV programme highlighted a problem over tainted tuna going on sale to the public. It was claimed that large quantities of the fish had been authorised for public sale by Minister of Fisheries and Oceans John Fraser. Inspectors found a particular brand had in fact been declared 'unfit for human consumption'.

Fraser defended his decision by accusing inspectors of being far too strict and of incomplete tests. Eventually the brand was withdrawn from the whole country and Fraser resigned, although he made a comeback

(Kieran Hughes)

as Speaker of the House soon afterwards. Meanwhile, questions were asked about how much Brian Mulroney knew about what was happening, although the PM insisted that he knew nothing about the problems until the story broke.

The pepper spray scandal

In 1997, Royal Canadian Mounted Police were accused of being heavy-handed after using pepper spray on protesting students in Vancouver. They were angry at the presence of Indonesian President Suharto at the APEC (Asia-Pacific Economic Cooperation) meeting in British Columbia. The protests were centred on Indonesia's alleged human rights abuses. Students were arrested for protesting and detained without any charges. They complained of the agony of the pepper spray, which felt like acid being thrown over them. Critics of the government said the way the students were treated was all about putting economics over the right to protest. Canadian Prime Minister Jean Chrétien, who served from 1993 to 2003, is a man prone to verbal gaffes in

Prince Philip style. He flippantly answered critics of the incident by saying: 'For me, pepper, I put it on my plate.' A public inquiry later said the Mounted Police had been at fault and that the Canadian government had interfered with the police operation.

The Canadian cabinet minister and the spy

Mixing a Canadian government defence minister and an East German prostitute who was also an alleged KGB spy during the Cold War was never going to be a good thing, but that is exactly what happened during the Munsinger Affair. Pierre Sévigny, Associate Minister of National Defence, was apparently not the only senior politician in John Diefenbaker's government to have had sex with Gerda Munsinger while she was living in Ottawa. This was Canada's first serious political sex scandal. Sévigny had been seeing her from 1958 to 1961.

Once her background had been discovered, Munsinger was deported to East Germany and the scandal was kept quiet in political circles. The potential security breach had been a serious matter. Sévigny resigned in 1963. During a heated parliamentary exchange in 1966, the affair was brought up and the press pounced on the scandal. It dominated the newspapers for weeks and was probably the biggest scandal many people had ever witnessed in their country. Later, a royal commission criticised Diefenbaker's handling of the situation but said that it did not find a security breach.

CHECHNYA

A naughty video starring a 'lookalike' Chechen leader

Ramzan Kadyrov, Chechnya's pro-Moscow prime minister, became embroiled in an embarrassing sex scandal in 2006. As a devout Muslim who preached the moral high ground, he was made to look rather stupid. Kadyrov's people did not take seriously a poor quality video showing a man in a sauna with two prostitutes. However, the man looked exactly like Kadyrov. The mere gossip of 'is it him, isn't him' in the video damaged his carefully managed image. Kadyrov, married with children, had introduced elements of Sharia law (the moral code and religious law of Islam) to Chechnya in 2005 and portrayed himself as deeply religious and a man of authority. The question over the video did not help his reputation.

CHILE

General Pinochet's Caravan of Death

Approximately 3,000 people went missing or died under the Chilean military coup of 1973 and the seventeen years of Augusto Pinochet's rule. Many opponents were tortured or imprisoned, or both. A number of the country's military leaders were punished for not being cruel enough and were themselves tortured or jailed.

In addition to years of executions, torture and imprisonment, as well as the disappearance of many people, an event called the Caravan of Death had a profound effect. This was a particularly cruel Chilean Army death squad that flew by Puma helicopter to various garrisons to inspect prisoners before killing them. The unit was armed with knives, machine guns and grenades. At least seventy-two people (possibly nearer to 100) were killed and it remains one of the most notorious episodes of human rights abuse during Pinochet's military rule of Chile.

In October 1973, one military squad arrived in the Antofagasta Province and executed fifty-six people without the knowledge of the district governor, General Joaquin Lagos, who promptly resigned. During the attacks, senior military personnel ordered prisoners to be sliced up alive with a machete before being shot. The governor had a face-to-face showdown with Pinochet, which is widely credited for ending the weeks of suffering under the hands of the Caravan of Death. Its victims had been buried in unmarked graves and the former governor later said that he did not recover the bodies for relatives because he was too ashamed about what had happened. Lagos later described to the world what he had seen:

> They were torn apart. They were no longer human bodies. I wanted to at least put the bodies back together again, to leave them more decent, but you couldn't. They cut eyes out with daggers. They broke their jaws and legs. They shot them to pieces, first the legs, then the sexual organs, then the heart, all with machine guns.

Many of the Caravan of Death's victims had given themselves up quietly and posed no threat to the regime. It was killing, without mercy, just for the sake of it. The killings and kidnappings continued elsewhere in the country under the new regime. Augusto Pinochet was indicted in December 2002 in relation to the Caravan of Death but was never judged over the atrocities because he died four years later, under house arrest. Experts claim the Caravan of Death was about sending a warning shot to potential opponents of the regime, citizens or even military commanders and officers who considered stepping out of line.

According to some figures, the number of victims of the military dictatorship stands at 3,195, of whom 1,183 are listed as 'disappeared'. However, Pinochet supporters claim some of the so-called 'disappeared' were later found alive and well, or had died of unrelated causes. Some victims' families received state compensation but in 2008, Chilean officials said they would sue families who falsely claimed that their relatives went missing during the 1973-90 dictatorship.

In October 1988, there was a referendum to decide if Pinochet should be the only candidate in the presidential election. He was disappointed to learn that the answer from the people was a clear 'no'. The following year, Chile had a new president, Patricio Aylwin, and Pinochet remained as commander-in-chief of the army.

Pinochet's visit to Britain in 1994 to inspect a missile project saw him warmly welcomed by several members of John Major's government. Previously, Margaret Thatcher had been a supporter of Pinochet.

In 1998, Pinochet resigned as head of the Chilean Army and became a senator, which gave him parliamentary immunity for life. In theory, he could not be punished for any atrocities carried out during his leadership. However, later that year he visited Britain once again and was arrested by police. This was a result of a request by judges investigating the disappearance of Spanish citizens during his time in office.

Law Lords decided that he should be sent to Spain but in January 2000, the British Home Secretary, Jack Straw, gave permission for him to return to Chile on compassionate grounds. Once he was back, proceedings against him started but were halted in 2001 because of his dementia. In 2005, the United States claimed Pinochet had embezzled $28 million during his time in office. He died in December 2006.

FRANCE

The French orgies

Not much is known about this scandal as it has not been documented very well. However, in 1958 the French nation was horrified by a sex scandal involving several well-known people and a group of young girls. The 'Ballets Roses' operated in a fashionable country house near Paris. The house was owned by a senior French politician named Le Troquer. He was an important political figure at the time, as he was president of the National Assembly. He also played an important role throughout the events of May-June 1958 that marked the return of General de Gaulle to power. During the famous Ballets Roses the girls performed various erotic ballets to entertain politicians and celebrities of both sexes. The dance routines often ended in orgies. The girls were aged between fifteen and seventeen. Le Troquer was charged in connection with child offences and received a nominal punishment.

Qui est le papa, François Mitterand?

Mitterand (b.1916 d.1996) was President of France from 1981–95. Despite being married to Danielle for more than five decades, he strayed many times. However, one of his liaisons

(Chris Hubbard)

stood out from the crowd, for two reasons. Firstly, his mistress Anne Pingeot got an apartment and presidential security protection, paid for by the French taxpayers. Secondly, and the bigger part of the scandal, he got Pingeot pregnant. His daughter, Mazarine, was born in 1974 and was kept a secret for many years.

In 1994, a media circus developed after the identity of Mitterand's illegitimate daughter became public. It was a major scandal of the day. Mitterand died of prostate cancer in 1996, aged seventy-nine. It is thought that he had first been diagnosed with cancer in 1981. Anne and Mazarine Pingeot showed up at his funeral. They had been invited by Mitterand's wife Danielle, who seated them next to the family.

Mitterand survived a number of scandals and remained popular throughout his career. The scandals first broke in the early 1990s in relation to his party's questionable funding schemes. His alleged role in a number of financial scandals involving French multinationals came to light, as well as the bombing of Greenpeace's environmental campaigning ship *Rainbow Warrior* in 1985 (when one of the campaigners was killed) and allegations that he sanctioned torture during Algeria's War of Independence of 1954-62.

GERMANY

Death of a German politician under investigation

Jürgen W. Möllemann, the former leader of Germany's liberals, died in 2003 when making a parachute jump. Police said it was an apparent suicide. Shortly before his death he had been accused of being involved in illegal arms deals and tax evasion. He was also being investigated over party funding rules, fraud and breach of trust. In 2002 he had made anti-Semitic comments and criticised Israeli and German Jewish leaders. Möllemann was elected to parliament in 1972 and served as education minister and later economics minister under former Chancellor Helmut Kohl.

Investigators claimed that the 57-year-old former army parachutist opened the parachute and cut it free from his body, subsequently falling to his death. There had apparently been nothing wrong with his parachute but further details were not released at the time. Möllemann had been part of a small group of parachutists who had jumped from 13,000 feet; the others all landed safely. Had he cut the parachute or tampered with the safety mechanism, or had someone else done that? Perhaps it had been a freak accident.

A former colleague of Möllemann refused to believe the suicide theory, despite his friend's difficulties. He said that Möllemann had been a fighter and would have contested the allegations against him. A number of other people had also been under the spotlight over various allegations at the time.

HUNGARY

Dunagate

Dunagate was obviously not quite as famous as America's Watergate scandal, but nonetheless a major scandal in Hungary in 1990. It was to result in a government investigation, various street protests and possibly a poor election result for socialists as a form of protest. It involved wiretapping of political enemies by the Communist government's secret services, as well as the shredding of sensitive documents and secret filming and collecting of information on activists and political leaders. It was pre-Berlin Wall collapse behaviour *after* the wall had come down. Evidence was released to the press that these political intrusions were still happening in the new 'free' state.

INDIA

Sex scandal, ice cream and Indian politicians

This seems like a strange mix of words but is it possible to put them all into just one sentence? An Indian ice cream parlour has been accused of being a front for a brothel run by a number of Indian politicians, judicial officers and other VIPs in a major sex scandal. You really couldn't make this up if you tried!

Accusations first emerged in 1997 that a certain ice cream parlour situated in Kerala was indeed a brothel. The allegations that, behind the Mr Whippy machine there were dubious paid-for sexual activities going on, caused hot debate in the country, especially when a few well-known politicians were linked to the running of the popular establishment. During one particular debate in the Kerala Assembly in 2011 when allegations were being put forward and then denied, absolute chaos erupted and proceedings had to be suspended. In addition, members of the Kerala government were accused of deliberately obstructing the investigation to protect themselves or their contacts.

Ice cream + sex = scandal. (Kieran Hughes)

INDONESIA

Once, twice ... three times caught on camera

Here are details of three separate sex scandals, two involving politicians and one that affected the political debates of the day.

Indonesian authorities remained rather secretive in 2011 in relation to a sex tape allegedly involving two politicians from the country's opposition party. It was suggested that the man and woman were both married but not to each other. The graphic video was somehow leaked onto the internet and the site was immediately blocked. The government's line remained vague about whether it was 'these people' in the video or not and promised further investigations. A number of people stepped forward to criticise the release of the video as political point-scoring. It came at a time when sex tapes were a sensitive issue. The country had already been divided over such behaviour after a leaked sex tape of top singer Nazril 'Ariel' Irham became widely available on the internet. He was arrested in June 2010 and eventually sent to jail after the tape of his sexual conquests had apparently been stolen from him. The morality of the mostly Muslim nation was under attack and there were protests on the streets, with some demanding Sharia law. At the time, President Susilo Bambang Yudhoyono said on television:

> If we don't care about these things, if we don't pay attention to decent clothes, for example, then we run the risk that scandals like this happen. This has nothing to do with freedom but it has to do with being appropriate, with politeness not to disturb other people. So please let's guard the morality of our nation because this is embarrassing, especially if people abroad see it too.

Finally, in April 2011 a conservative Indonesian lawmaker stepped down after an embarrassing incident concerning his enjoyment of porn at work! In Britain we often complain when it appears that certain members of the House of Lords are asleep during proceedings, but this Indonesian lawmaker was caught watching a porn film on his computer in the middle of a parliamentary debate. He was caught on camera enjoying the adult flick and so could not deny it. The 50-year-old issued an apology and immediately stepped down. He had been one of those politicians who had helped push through anti-porn laws in the country in 2008.

The 2008 legislation had faced furious opposition and protest from some of the non-Muslim minority (who number about 10 per cent of the population). Islamic parties defended the law, saying it was a vital tool in the protection of women and children against immorality and exploitation. Images, talk and gestures seen as pornographic all came under the new laws. Many took to the streets to support the new laws under discussion, worried about moral degeneration in their country. Others, of several religions, just called for greater controls. But since the new laws came into effect there has definitely been evidence of double standards.

IRAN

The chain murders in Iran
Between 1988 and 1998, dozens of writers, political activists, religious converts, doctors, priests, intellectuals and ordinary citizens were murdered or simply disappeared in Iran, a whole chain of them. They were stabbed, shot, poisoned or were victims of staged robberies. They had all been critical of the Islamic republic in some way and paid for it with their lives.

Who the perpetrators of these crimes were has always been disputed. The country's Supreme Leader Ayatollah Ali Khamenei denied that the government was behind any of the murders. He blamed enemies of Iran. Iranian officials conveniently blamed a rogue – and conveniently dead – intelligence officer. A number of other intelligence officers were sent to prison in 2001 or sentenced to death. Critics were suspicious and suggested the accused villains were merely scapegoats for the government attempting to suppress any opposition. One of the newspaper editors who pursued the story was found shot in the head in 2000, although he survived the shooting.

There remains an element of secrecy and uncertainty over the killings. In 1994, writers publicly demanded an end to government censorship. Many of those who had signed an open letter in the press were found dead in suspicious circumstances. The website iranhumanity.com calls for charges in relation to crimes against humanity.

ISRAEL

A bad day for humanity

A young American woman named Rachel Corrie was a civil rights campaigner who was crushed to death by an Israeli bulldozer in March 2003. The 23-year-old activist had been demonstrating to stop the demolition of homes in the Gaza Strip with the pro-Palestinian International Solidarity Movement. A witness claimed that Rachel had been clearly visible on a mound of earth and it would have been impossible not to have seen her.

The scandal continues in the investigation into Rachel's death that was launched afterwards. An Israeli judge decided Rachel had put herself in danger. Her parents claim that Rachel's death had been completely avoidable and that the Israeli government should have been more accountable for what happened. Rachel's parents are adamant that the investigation protected the Israeli military. Her supporters claimed a culture of impunity over fairness and, at a press conference in 2012 after hearing the verdict, vowed to continue their fight for justice. Rachel's mother, Cindy, called the day Israel cleared itself of any fault 'a bad day not only for our family, but a bad day for human rights, for humanity, for the rule of law and also for the country of Israel'. Some would certainly argue that this was a whitewash or scandal, or both. A lawsuit filed by Corrie's parents, from Olympia, Washington State, accused the Israeli military of either unlawfully or intentionally killing Rachel. The lawsuit also accused the military of gross negligence. The family sued for a symbolic $1 in damages. They lost their case when an Israeli judge said the State of Israel was not responsible and dismissed a civil lawsuit. The judge said that Corrie's death was not caused by the negligence of the Israeli state or army and claimed that the driver of the bulldozer that killed her could not have seen her.

Moshe Katsav's rape and harassment trial

It is not often a country's president is sent to prison but this is exactly what happened in Israel in 2011. Moshe Katsav was forced to step down after a number of female employees accused him of sexual harassment. One woman accused him of rape and the case went to court in the country's highest-profile case ever. He rejected a plea bargain that would have allowed him to avoid jail and instead demanded he was innocent and that he would be able to prove it, but he was given a seven-year jail sentence for raping a former aide and molesting two other women who worked for him. An appeal was unsuccessful and Israel's Supreme Court upheld the sentence. The court accused Katsav of misusing his high position and he was put behind bars. His attorneys appealed for leniency and Katsav broke down in tears, claiming the girls had all lied and the sentence was a great injustice.

The 65-year-old Katsav, who was president from 2000 to 2007, was convicted of twice raping an aide when he was a cabinet minister in the late 1990s. The sexual assaults against the other two women happened during his presidency. His fall from grace was spectacular: from president to inmate in a matter of months. Katsav resigned under public pressure just a few weeks before his term was to end. The position of presidency in Israel is largely ceremonial and filled by an elder statesman figure; a man who should be above politics and who could hold the country together. The president is not, however, above the law and the judge made this clear. The functions of government continued almost undisturbed throughout the scandal.

The country had watched the whole case with great interest. Katsav had many supporters; some from his home town of Kiryat Malachi. At the same time there were many women (and men) who visibly supported the women's claims. During the case many of them stood with banners outside the courtroom. There were angry clashes in the courtroom as well. After sentencing, the prime minister and opposition leader both issued carefully-worded statements that expressed sorrow for Katsav's fate but at the same time declaring respect for the sentences issued by the court. On 7 December 2011, Katsav arrived at the prison in Ramla to begin his sentence.

JAPAN

The Japanese HIV-tainted blood scandal

More than a thousand patients in Japan pursued the government and drug makers for damages over a twenty-year period following this scandal. It happened in the 1980s when up to 2,000 haemophilia patients in Japan contracted HIV through the use of unheated blood products after the development of heat treatments that prevented the spread of infection.

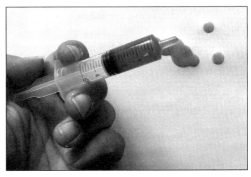
(Kieran Hughes)

There were legal implications for a number of officials in Japan's Ministry of Health and Welfare, as well as a doctor and several drug manufacturers. The first group of plaintiffs filed a damages suit back in 1989. In 1996, a landmark settlement was reached at the Tokyo District Court between more than 400 plaintiffs and the government and pharmaceutical companies. In 2011, lawyers claimed more than 1,300 plaintiffs had finally reached agreements with the defendants.

MEXICO

Dance of the forty-one ... or is it forty-two?

In 1901 in Mexico, police raided an illegal party at a private home and got slightly more than they had bargained for. What they were not expecting were forty-one (later suggested as forty-two after the president's son-in-law was allowed to slip away) men dressed as women, dancing and partying the night away. It was understood that the party included many senior politicians and VIPs, but the list of names was never published. The blushes were spared of the cross-dressing politicians, despite a court hearing. The wigs, false breasts, pretty jewellery, high heels and make-up were all taken away in exchange for a spell in the army. Homosexuality has often been referred to as '41 and 42' in Mexico's popular culture as a result of the scandal more than a hundred years ago.

The Mexican Towelgate Scandal

Expenses scandals have not been confined to the United Kingdom. Towelgate was the name of the expenses scandal of the Mexican government in 2001. The scandal centred on expenditure on the residence of the country's president, Vicente Fox.

The Mexican newspaper *Milenio* listed the extravagant spending habits of the presidential residence, including embroidered towels and bed sheets costing hundreds of dollars and decorating costing hundreds of thousands of dollars. It caused immense embarrassment to the administration and there were a number of senior resignations. To make matters worse, Fox had campaigned for office promising austerity in government and a cutback of excessive spending.

The president ordered an investigation and the chief government auditor went to work. He found a number of financial irregularities, overpricing and dubious invoices. Fox tried to turn the scandal to his advantage, pointing out that journalists only reported the facts because his government had been open and transparent and had put the figures in the public domain in the first place.

THE PHILIPPINES

The president, the actress, the angry first lady and martial law

American piano teacher turned B-movie actress Dovie Beams is perhaps known for her relationship with the Philippine President Ferdinand Marcos. She was in the country making a film that had been partially financed by Marcos and became his mistress between 1968 and 1970. Marcos was a well-known philanderer who had many affairs and is reputed to have seventeen illegitimate children from his various flings. Their break-up and allegations of a tape of their pillow talk together caused a major political scandal and seriously damaged Marcos's reputation. It became the cause of huge embarrassment to the president. Some say it was the trigger for martial law being brought in soon after, in 1972, to silence the opposition. Beams left the country in 1970, fearing for her safety. Imelda Marcos had become more aggressive after the affair had been revealed. Beams became a potential assassination target. Meanwhile, twelve of Marcos's closest advisers (usually military and police leaders) during the martial law period were given extra powers. Some were investigated over human rights issues, including torture, murder, seizures of property and displacement from homes. Political opponents were rounded up; schools were closed; and newspapers, TV and radio offices were seized by the military. Airline flights were suspended, as were international phone calls. Curfews were brought in and public demonstrations were banned.

The closest advisers who organised the crackdown became known as the Rolex 12 after stories of Marcos giving each of them a Rolex watch. It is widely thought, however, that this is a myth and that they each received either a fake or an ordinary watch. A number of these Marcos devotees fled with the president and his family when they were forced to flee in 1986.

Imelda Marcos and her shoes

The shoe museum holding many of Imelda's famous items of footwear. (Ronald Eric E. Mancesa)

Imelda Marcos had thousands of pairs of shoes. (Illustration by Bea Fox)

Imelda Marcos was known for her obsessive shoe buying and amassed a collection of thousands of pairs at a time when millions of ordinary Filipinos existed in extreme poverty.

Her husband died in exile but Imelda returned to the Philippines and settled there, even twice running unsuccessfully for president in later years and successfully for other political positions. Her husband's successor, Corazon Aquino, ordered the shoes to be put on show to demonstrate the extravagance of the former first lady. In 2001, Imelda opened her own museum in Marikina, the footwear capital of the Philippines.

Around 200,000 people work in Marikina and its shoe industry is evident in its road names, including Slipper Street and Sandal Street. The exact number of pairs of Imelda's shoes has been contested over the years. When the Marcoses fled to Hawaii when he was toppled from power, some of her shoes were left behind with other possessions. The figure is usually thought to be between 1,000 and 3,000 pairs.

PORTUGAL

Portugal's bloody political power struggle

The Távora affair was an eighteenth-century Portuguese power struggle between King Joseph I of Portugal, his prime minister, Sebastião de Melo, and the country's nobility. The events followed a massive earthquake in Lisbon in November 1755, when the king and his family were forced into a community of barracks and tents following the destruction of the royal palace. The royal family was surrounded by their servants, advisers and nobility. The old aristocrats and the prime minister were arch-enemies and the king was in the middle of many of the disagreements.

The king's favourite mistress was Teresa Leonor, wife of Luis Bernardo. He was heir of the powerful and influential Távora family, well-connected and politically active. One night in September 1758, Joseph I was returning from an evening of fun and frolics with his mistress in a plain, unmarked carriage, when he was attacked by armed men and shot, but not fatally. The king and his driver made it back to the tented community.

The prime minister was furious that an attempt had been made on the king's life. The question was, had this been a planned attack on the king or was it a random attack on a carriage travelling near Lisbon? Sebastião de Melo immediately launched an investigation and claimed to have apprehended the suspects soon after. Two men were hanged for the attack on the king but de Melo claimed the men confessed that they had been following orders of the Távora family. De Melo claimed that he had learnt how the Távora family were planning to put the Duke of Aveiro on the throne.

The Marchioness Leonor of Távora, her husband and several generations of their extended family were thrown in jail. They were accused of being linked to the attempted regicide of King Joseph I. In 1759, most of the family were put to death, burnt at the stake or decapitated. Some were tortured publicly first by having their arms and legs broken. It was a screaming, bloody and cruel scene of suffering, witnessed by the king. Some reports suggest that his advisers and servants were horrified and mystified by the extremity of the executions. No doubt they were too scared to protest.

Some of the women and children were eventually spared through the intervention of the queen. Their homes were destroyed and lands salted so nothing would ever grow there. Then the land was confiscated by the Crown. Had Sebastião de Melo set up the old aristocracy to get rid of them once and for all? Historians are divided over whether or not the Távora family was involved in a plot to kill the king. There was certainly a lack of evidence. Perhaps de Melo was so politically influential he managed to persuade the king that this had been the only option. The end result of this story came about because of the political interference on the balance of power between king, nobility and prime minister. De Melo enjoyed incredible political power for the remainder of Joseph's reign. When Joseph's daughter Maria I succeeded, she sacked him but did not punish him for what many saw as his persecution of the nobility. Many had demanded he be punished.

Today the site of the field where the torture and executions took place is a square called Terreiro Salgado. There is a small memorial there, just a few feet high, which for many effectively turned into a urinating spot. Sebastião de Melo was made Count of Oeiras and later Marquis of Pombal. His descendants still hold the titles today.

RUSSIA

The Russian backhanders

In 1999, the then Russian president, Boris Yeltsin, was accused of taking bribes from a construction company. Swiss investigators claimed that the president and certain senior government officials pocketed millions of dollars from a company that wanted to win key Kremlin contracts. The Kremlin said that the allegations were simply not true. Swiss investigators claimed that those responsible for offering the bribes did so over several years, paying them into separate bank accounts and giving credit cards. Figures banded about ranged from millions, and even billions, of dollars. The Russian authorities announced they were launching their own investigation. There were accusations of money laundering through a number of foreign companies and bank accounts.

Or maybe the biggest-ever US-Russian scandal was when Yeltsin was a guest at the White House and drank so much he was found outside in his underpants, hailing a cab to go and buy a pizza. It almost caused an international incident!

The cheating Russian parliamentary vote

In 2010, the Russian parliament was put to shame during a vote on drink–driving laws. Only eighty-eight out of 450 members of the Duma, Russia's lower house of parliament, were present for the vote. However, when it came to pressing the button by their seat to place their vote the deputies ran from empty seat to empty seat, kindly voting in place of absent colleagues. The bizarre episode was filmed and the scandalous, cheating antics went viral on the internet for the whole world to see. The vote was passed by more than 99 per cent.

Sex, drugs, tapes and lies

It sounds rather like the plot of a James Bond film, but this was real-life Russian politics. During the Cold War, the KGB was known for entrapping CIA officers with sexy female spies, filming them and blackmailing them, compromising US intelligence. The 'honeytrap' is nothing new; it has been used many times, inside and outside of politics.

It still goes on today, decades after the fall of the Berlin Wall and the end of the Cold War. The modern-day Kremlin has used honeytraps to discredit critics of Vladimir Putin. A beautiful model called Katya has starred in videotaped epics of sex and drugs with Putin's critics. One victim caught on videotape was Ilya Yashin, leader of the anti-Putin Solidarity Party, a single man in his twenties. He did suspect foul play quite early on in the trap, before too much had

The political power of the honeytrap. (Kieran Hughes)

happened, especially when Katya wanted him to have some cocaine. Despite leaving the room quickly, there was enough on tape to ruin him and it was played publicly over and over again. Katya managed to ensnare several other critics, including a National Bolshevik Party member, a television writer who mocked the Putin government and an anti-Putin singer.

SINGAPORE

Underage call girls and the officials

Singapore prides itself on having legalised prostitution in order to bring it under government control and squeeze out the criminal element through careful monitoring and tight regulations. Singapore's sex industry dates back to the days of the British Empire.

However, a scandal involving underage call girls, businessmen and civil servants emerged in 2012. A total of forty-eight men were charged under 2008 legislation that makes it illegal to pay for sex with a girl under the age of eighteen. The allegations centred round a girl who was seventeen years old at the time of doing business. The under-age call girl scandal was a huge embarrassment for the government because of the country's clean-living image.

SOMALIA

Fighting, fleeing, famine and then, finally, free elections

In August 2012, elections in Somalia signalled a much-needed new beginning after the country had been embroiled in a devastating twenty-year civil war. There had been a number of failed attempts to create a unitary government but the August 2012 elections were seen as a new beginning after years of disaster. Despite the huge step forward there were still claims of corruption, intimidation and political interference in the new political process and selection.

The country wants to replace famine, war, anarchy, corruption, embezzlement and scandal with a proper constitution, stability, reforms and regulation. During the years of war, people fled the country and many businesses relocated to Kenya. Meanwhile, Somalia became synonymous with piracy, with several attacks on innocent seafarers along the coast. The European Union used warships and put armed guards on ships under Operation Atalanta, which started in 2008. Most of the piracy has been linked to the Puntland region, which is rife with anarchy and lawlessness.

A number of autonomous and semi-autonomous states emerged in Somalia after the civil war in the early 1990s. President Mohamed Siad Barre was overthrown in 1991. Rival militia fought for control and thousands of people starved or fled as the country was ripped apart through a political and factional struggle, with clan-on-clan fighting under many different warlords. During the factional fighting, escalated violence and worsening humanitarian situation over the years, more than a million people have been internally displaced and more than half a million others have fled to neighbouring countries such as Kenya, Yemen and Ethiopia. Various aid agencies have attempted to assist people with emergency relief items and shelters as and when security conditions have allowed them to get near the displaced people. In 2011, millions were at risk because of a lack of water. The United Nations reported a very serious drought in the country.

There was hope in 2004 with the formation of the Transitional Federal Government, which stayed in place until the 2012 elections. A significant and historical date in the country's history was 20 August 2012, as the first parliament in more than twenty years sat in Mogadishu, with new women MPs as well as men. Political advances throughout the rest of the country will no doubt follow. Meanwhile, a special committee removed MPs who had been linked to violence and corruption, and police in Mogadishu remained on alert to assist with the smooth running of the all-important election after militant Islamists had been chased out. The presidential election was held

Presidential campaigning at Mogadishu, August 2012. (Nazanine Moshiri)

Somali journalists waiting for the new MPs' swearing-in ceremony at Mogadishu, August 2012. (Nazanine Moshiri)

New women MPs at Mogadishu, August 2012. (Nazanine Moshiri)

From left to right: the country's Chief Justice Aidid Abdullahi Ilkahanaf, President Sheikh Sharif (centre) and Augustine Mahiga, Head of the United Nations Political Office for Somalia, a few days before the parliamentary election in August 2012, and several weeks before the presidential election. (Nazanine Moshiri)

Somali police (including a female officer), keeping events running smoothly. (Nazanine Moshiri)

several weeks later on 10 September 2012, when Hassan Sheikh Mohamud was elected as the new president of Somalia.

The following photographs from Mogadishu have been reproduced by kind permission of international journalist Nazanine Moshiri.

SOUTH AFRICA

The mayor and the porn sites
As far back as 2000, when the internet was relatively new in the workplace, some people realised that not all porn had been blocked by certain IT departments. Surely nobody would be stupid enough to look at adult sites at work though? Well, the Reverend – that's right – William Bantom did just that, while he was Mayor of Cape Town. He was in office from 1995 to 2000 and was also a

(Bridget Hughes)

minister of the Church of Nazarene. He was the city's first black mayor after the new post-apartheid multi-racial elections in 1995.

Bantom had been caught once already and given another chance. The first time he said it was part of his research for a thesis he was working on but when pushed by officials, he broke down and promised it would not happen again. The second time, the 54-year-old father of two admitted doing wrong, resigned and asked for forgiveness from the community. Later, the council put an automatic stop on all adult sites.

SPAIN

Corruption in Spain, again, again and again …

Spain has long been associated with various political scandals and in recent years hundreds of mayors and other important government officials have been investigated for bribery and other misdemeanours, with some having assets frozen too. According to America's NPR News network, between 2005 and 2010, Spain's Interior Ministry said that nearly a thousand people had been arrested in various anti-corruption probes throughout the country. In addition, assets worth in excess of $4 billion had been seized.

Many of these scandals revolved around local mayors having too much power and influence, and questions have been asked about the concession of building permits and the awarding of contracts to organise public events, including state visits. Many ordinary citizens lost their faith in politics during the difficult Franco dictatorship from 1939 to 1975. Today, many politicians in Spain want to clean up the country's politics. However, the Spanish people have at times seen some of their politicians arrested for bribery, misuse of public funds and even money laundering. Spain has thousands of professional politicians, at a cost of more than €700 million a year in wages, all courtesy of the taxpayer. According to one poll, more than 85 per cent of Spaniards believe corruption in Spain is 'very widespread' and more than one-third say it is merely part of Spanish culture. Even the Spanish newspapers have been full of articles asking why there is so much corruption in the country. One news report in 2011 claimed that there were as many as 700 cases being investigated by the country's Ministry of Justice, involving all forty-eight provinces.

There are many theories about why Spain is so corrupt, ranging from religion to greed and local competition to revenge for the years of dictatorship. Many politicians believe that others are more corrupt than themselves. Nobody knows for sure how Spanish politics got into such a mess, but it did. There have been lots of newspaper articles and books written around the world about Spain's political corruption.

Meanwhile, there is the ongoing trouble of British people buying property in Spain, legally, through established lawyers in the country, and finding out later that their property is in fact 'illegal'. Also, unscrupulous developers, with dodgy politicians, have taken land from private owners and forced them to contribute to the cost of developing it. Scandalous Spanish politicians have done little to stop this practice, despite condemnation from the EU. This seems like a problem that will not go away despite all the bad publicity for Spain. Many ex-pats have lost thousands of pounds in the scandal.

SWAZILAND

Not enough wives to go round?

In 2011 it was reported that King Mswati III of Swaziland had thrown his justice minister into jail for sleeping with one of his fourteen royal wives. You'd think he would not have minded as there were so many to go around – two for each day of the week – but he minded! Still, it is probably not the wisest move for a politician to sleep with the king's wife, even if he has lots of them.

The Swaziland monarch's rule is absolute in this small southern African state; he is all-powerful and believes in his traditional tribal practice of polygamy. Each year, hundreds of the country's unmarried women are paraded before the king so he can pick another 'lucky' girl to wed and bed. Press are banned from reporting such goings-on as royal adultery in this tiny country, so some of the rumours no doubt get a little out of hand.

The offending royal wife will spend the rest of her life under twenty-four-hour surveillance, but should feel lucky as her lover contemplates his actions behind bars.

SWEDEN

The Kejne affair

In 1948 in Sweden, Pastor Karl-Erik Kejne accused various groups of homosexual men of trying to threaten and kill him. The pastor had previously tried to get a ban on Stockholm's gay prostitution trade. He also accused gay criminal gangs of being organised by a gay mafia. He then accused a senior politician of trying to trick him into being 'outed' himself by sending a pretend gay honeytrap to his house. The whole event was played out in the newspapers and was a big scandal at the time. Although homosexuality had been legalised in Sweden in 1944, it was still not seen as a socially acceptable way of life until the 1950s.

SWITZERLAND

The Swiss government and the 'missing' millions

Since the end of the Second World War, the worldwide Jewish community and family and descendants of Jews killed in the Holocaust have been trying reclaim their money from Swiss banks. Before the war, many prominent Jews had put their wealth into the Swiss banking system to keep it away from the Nazis. Those that perished had left behind their wealth, which sat comfortably in Swiss bank accounts. Many Swiss banks also held accounts for the Nazis.

After the end of the Second World War, the Swiss government sat back for years and did very little while the families of those who had died tried to reclaim the money. The Swiss government let its nation's banks run circles round those trying to reclaim what had been 'stolen' from them. Victims' families might remember that a relative had hidden wealth in Swiss banks but did not have account numbers. To make matters worse, Swiss banks insisted on a death certificate for deceased relatives. Of course, those who perished in the Holocaust never had death certificates.

The Swiss government ordered an investigation into various aspects of Swiss conduct during and after the war and claimed it had discovered evidence of the Swiss central bank buying Nazi gold and of Jewish refugees being cruelly turned away from Swiss borders at their time of need. However, it should be remembered that other countries also turned away Jewish people on the run.

Over the years, victims complained about being drowned in paperwork from certain Swiss banks, being ignored and offered much smaller sums than had been owed, which resulted in stress and upset and the health of victims being affected. However, an investigation found no proof that banks had been destroying records of Holocaust victims' accounts or that they had used the money for improper purposes. Investigators claimed that a conspiracy had existed among the Swiss banks to stonewall heirs of Holocaust survivors who had made claims to Swiss bank accounts.

The Swiss National Bank openly carried out gold transactions during the war but a Swiss government study carried out by a board of academics in the 1990s declared that its business did not prolong the war. This declaration came out despite Hitler's war efforts being partly funded through the value of confiscated Nazi gold being put on the open market, facilitated by the Swiss banking system. Perhaps the Swiss government should today ask itself whether it is sure that any gold transacted during or just after the Second World War does not contain the gold fillings or wedding rings of those Jews exterminated in the death camps. A long-running legal battle came to an end in 1998, but there followed objections to the fairness of the settlement and various agreements. It wasn't until 2001 that everything was resolved, and the distributions process really began.

TAIWAN

A politician's intimate moments released on DVD

Chu Mei-feng, a former Taipei city councillor, left office in 2001 after video footage was released of her having sex with her married lover. The footage had been secretly recorded by a so-called 'friend', who she later sued, and was then widely circulated to millions of people and sent to a popular weekly tabloid-style magazine called *Scoop*. The magazine also gave away copies of the film on DVD. The friend who had secretly installed the camera in the bedroom was jailed, and the magazine also got into trouble. At the time, the government pulled the DVD from shop shelves, claiming that the publishers had broken laws relating to indecent material. This action made the DVD even more popular and copies were sold on the black market throughout the country as well as in neighbouring countries.

Police officers apparently found ten different recording devices hidden about Chu's home, in her office and even in her car. The 'intrusion' into her private life and whether the press had overstepped privacy boundaries became a popular moral debate throughout the country. For weeks it seemed that nobody was talking about anything else.

After the scandal, she became a successful singer and went on tour, although she was banned from performing in Malaysia because of the sex video. People in Singapore indulged in a moral debate over whether she was cashing in on the scandal and the Singapore authorities fined a television station more than $5,000 for broadcasting an excerpt from the sex tape, even though crucial parts were blanked out.

Chu later returned to Taiwan and changed career yet again. In 2007 she was hired as a TV news reporter. She started broadcasting at 6.30 pm on Macau Asian Satellite TV (MASTV) on 20 March. In a bizarre induction ceremony, the TV channel tried to separate Chu's former troubles from her new venture by getting her to step over a basin of fire dressed in a red wedding gown and veil to drive away bad luck. In February 2002, she capitalised on the publicity by releasing her autobiography, *Confessions of Chu Mei-feng*. Meanwhile, pirated discs had already been widely circulated in Taiwan, China and the United States. Chu never denied that she was the woman in the film and she publicly apologised.

Taiwanese president caught with his hands in the till
This was a spectacular fall from grace of gargantuan proportions. Chen Shui-bian was elected president of Taiwan in 2000. He served in office for eight years but ended up in prison. His reputation was first tarnished by his son-in-law with allegations of insider trading. His popularity certainly took a battering following the scandal and his approval ratings dipped to almost 5 per cent. In 2008, other members of his family got into trouble, and the president himself was also named in the proceedings. Shui-bian's wife, son and daughter-in-law were accused of a number of crimes, including embezzlement and money laundering. Shui-bian was accused of wiring $20 million to several different bank accounts using false names. In the end, his dishonesty caught up with him and his family. Chen Shui-bian and his wife were both fined $15 million, with life imprisonment too. The sentence was later reduced to twenty years.

TURKEY

Kaya Village, the Turkish ghost town
The governments of Turkey and Greece failed to efficiently complete a population exchange in the 1920s. There had been an agreement between them over a population exchange where the Greek people in Turkey would return to Greece and the Turkish people in Greece would return to Turkey. Although the Greek people from Kaya (originally called Levissi) went back to Greece, the Turkish people in Greece refused to go back to Turkey without compensation for the lands that they were leaving behind. So the houses back in Turkey sat empty as the politicians failed to manage and take control of the situation. The stand-off was never fully resolved and the houses in Kaya stood empty from 1923, rotting away, deserted, lonely and abandoned. This housing estate has now become a tourist attraction and people can wander around the estate and through the crumbling properties, where animals graze and nature has taken possession.

Today, Kaya Village is composed of approximately 1,000 houses, two schools and two churches, all built on a steep mountainside. The houses were built by local skilled workmen and designed so each home does not directly overlook another. All the buildings remain in a partly demolished state. Kaya has now been declared an historical monument and has become a popular tourist attraction.

How Kaya Village looks today: deserted, crumbling and neglected. (Bridget Hughes)

Chapter Four

Miscellany

What is it with governments and cars?

Here are two examples of governments 'taking' cars …

Firstly, in the Philippines, President Estrada's 'Customs Bureau' seized several luxury smuggled cars and SUVs. The assignment of these vehicles to favoured allies and supporters was exposed by a local politician in Venezuela City, in the Philippines. There were calls for the president to return the 'hot cars' to the country's Bureau. The president rejected the idea initially but later agreed that the cars could be sold properly, through auction. The Hot Cars Scandal might have been a lot hotter had he failed to back down over pressure to sell the vehicles through the appropriate channels.

Secondly, the UK government has in the past been accused of seizing cars at ports and selling them at auction, even while an appeal by the rightful

(Bruno Brookes)

owner to have the vehicle returned was in progress. The seizing of cars has often centred round discrepancies or disagreements over incorrect amounts of alcohol and tobacco being brought back from 'booze runs', as opposed to smuggled cars previously mentioned. When UK customs officers seize goods, they can also seize the vehicle too. A number of television programmes have highlighted this scandal. When working in television I had the pleasure of interviewing the government minister in charge of the searches at ports, but I had arranged to discuss an unrelated matter. I was warned by his aide not to mention these political allegations about car seizures. Having been convinced that we still had free speech in the UK, I challenged him at the end of the interview. He denied that any of this went on, despite case studies being published in the national press that week of people seeing their cars seized and sold.

Chapter Five

Great Political Quotes

Politics is the art of looking for trouble, finding it everywhere, diagnosing it incorrectly and applying the wrong remedies.

Groucho Marx, comedian and film and television star.

Don't fall in love with politicians; they're all a disappointment. They can't help it, they just are.

Peggy Noonan, author.

Politicians and diapers should be changed frequently and all for the same reason.
José Maria de Eça de Queiróz, Portuguese writer, translated from Portuguese.

We'd all like to vote for the best man, but he's never a candidate.

Frank McKinney Hubbard, cartoonist.

Those who are too smart to engage in politics are punished by being governed by those who are dumber.

Plato, philosopher.

George Washington is the only president who didn't blame the previous administration for his troubles.

Unknown.

If God had been a Liberal there wouldn't have been Ten Commandments; there would have been Ten Suggestions.

Malcolm Bradbury, writer.

How come we choose from just two people to run for president and fifty for Miss America?
Unknown.

We hang the petty thieves and appoint the great ones to public office. Everyone knows politics is a contact sport.

Barack Obama, US president.

I used to say that politics was the second-oldest profession. I have come to know that it bears a gross similarity to the first.

Ronald Reagan, former US president.

Ten people who speak make more noise than 10,000 who are silent.
> Napoleon Bonaparte, political and military leader of France.

Everything is changing. People are taking their comedians seriously and the politicians as a joke.
> Will Rogers, writer, actor and broadcaster.

For seven and a half years I've worked alongside President Reagan. We've had triumphs, made some mistakes. We've had some sex ... uh ... setbacks.
> George Bush Sr, former US president.

Outside of the killings, Washington has one of the lowest crime rates in the country.
> Marion Barry, former mayor of Washington, DC.

I've looked on many women with lust. I've committed adultery in my heart many times. God knows I will do this and forgives me.
> Jimmy Carter, former US president.

A politician thinks of the next election; a statesman thinks of the next generation.
> James Freeman Clarke, theologian and scholar.

Democracy is being allowed to vote for the candidate you dislike least.
> Robert Byrne, author.

It is not in the nature of politics that the best men should be elected. The best men do not want to govern their fellow men.
> George MacDonald, writer.

I've now been in fifty-seven states; I think one left to go.
> Barack Obama, US president.

Stand up, Chuck, let 'em see ya.
> Joe Biden, US vice-president, in front of an election rally crowd, to Missouri State Senator Chuck Graham, who is in a wheelchair.

So what?
> President George W. Bush, former US president, responding to an ABC News correspondent who pointed out that Al Qaeda wasn't a threat in Iraq until after the US invaded.

Making a speech on economics is a bit like pissing down your leg. It seems hot to you but never to anyone else.

> Lyndon B. Johnson, former US president.

Blessed are the young, for they shall inherit the National Debt.

> Herbert Hoover, former US president.

The world will not accept dictatorship or domination.

> Mikhail Gorbachev, former president of the Soviet Union.

On Margaret Thatcher: *The eyes of Caligula, the mouth of Marilyn Monroe.*

> François Mitterand, former French president.

The most dangerous thing about student riots is that adults take them seriously.

> Georges Pompidou, former French president.

Richard Nixon is a no good, lying bastard. He can lie out of both sides of his mouth at the same time, and if he ever caught himself telling the truth, he'd lie just to keep his hand in.

> Harry S. Truman, former US president.

Don't get excited about a tax cut. It's like a mugger giving you back fare for a taxi.

> Arnold Glasgow, humourist.

Apart from that Mrs Lincoln, how did you enjoy the play?

> Tom Lehrer, songwriter, musician, lecturer and mathematician.

The president has kept all the promises he intended to keep.

> Clinton aide George Stephanopoulos.

All the president is, is a glorified public relations man who spends his time flattering, kissing, and kicking people to get them to do what they are supposed to do anyway.

> Harry S. Truman, former US president.

I am extraordinarily patient, provided I get my own way in the end.

> Margaret Thatcher, former British prime minister.

Bad politicians are sent to Washington by good people who don't vote.

> William E. Simon, former politician and philanthropist.

I should prefer to have a politician who regularly went to a massage parlour than one who promised a laptop computer for every teacher.

> A.N. Wilson, journalist and author.

If the United States of America or Britain is having elections, they don't ask for observers from Africa or from Asia. But when we have elections, they want observers.
Nelson Mandela, former South African president.

If you put the federal government in charge of the Sahara Desert, in five years there'd be a shortage of sand.
Milton Friedman, economist, statistician, academic and author.

In politics nothing is contemptible.
Benjamin Disraeli, former British prime minister.

Healthy citizens are the greatest asset any country can have.
Winston Churchill, former British prime minister.

Whoever does not miss the Soviet Union has no heart; whoever wants it back has no brain.
Vladimir Putin, Russian president.

Jesus was the first socialist, the first to seek a better life for mankind.
Mikhail Gorbachev, former president of the Soviet Union.

Chapter Six

Who Were the Leaders?

British Prime Ministers 1721-2013

Sir Robert Walpole, 1721-42, Whig
Spencer Compton, 1st Earl of Wilmington, 1742-43, Whig
Henry Pelham, 1743-54, Whig
Thomas Pelham-Holles, Duke of Newcastle, 1754-56, Whig
William Cavendish, Duke of Devonshire, 1756-57, Whig
Thomas Pelham-Holles, Duke of Newcastle, 1757-62, Whig
John Stuart, Earl of Bute, 1762-63, Tory
George Grenville, 1763-65, Whig
Charles Watson-Wentworth, Marquess of Rockingham, 1765-66, Whig
William Pitt 'The Elder', Earl of Chatham, 1766-68, Whig
Augustus Henry Fitzroy, Duke of Grafton, 1768-70, Whig
Lord Frederick North, 1770-82, Tory
Charles Watson-Wentworth, Marquess of Rockingham, 1782, Whig
William Petty, Earl of Shelburne, 1782-83, Whig
William Bentinck, Duke of Portland, 1783, Whig
William Pitt 'The Younger', 1783-1801, Whig
Henry Addington, 1801-04, Tory
William Pitt 'The Younger', 1804-06, Tory
William Wyndham Grenville, Lord Grenville, 1806-07, nominally Tory
William Bentinck, Duke of Portland, 1807-09, Whig
Spencer Perceval, 1809-12, Tory
Robert Banks Jenkinson, Earl of Liverpool, 1812-27, Conservative
George Canning, 1827, Tory
Frederick Robinson, Viscount Goderich, 1827-28, Tory
Arthur Wellesley, Duke of Wellington, 1828-30, Tory
Earl Grey, 1830-34, Whig
William Lamb, Viscount Melbourne, 1834, Whig
Sir Robert Peel, 1834-35, Conservative
William Lamb, Viscount Melbourne, 1835-41, Whig
Arthur Wellesley, 1st Duke of Wellington, 1834, Tory

Sir Robert Peel, 1841-46, Conservative
Earl Russell, 1846-52, Whig
Edward Smith Stanley, Earl of Derby, 1852, Tory/Whig
George Hamilton Gordon, Earl of Aberdeen, 1852-55, Conservative
Henry John Temple, Viscount Palmerston, 1855-58, Tory/Whig
Edward Smith Stanley, Earl of Derby, 1858-59, Tory/Whig
Henry John Temple, Viscount Palmerston, 1859-65, Tory/Whig
Earl Russell, 1865-66, Whig
Edward Smith Stanley, Earl of Derby, 1866-68, Tory/Whig
Benjamin Disraeli, 1868, Conservative
William Ewart Gladstone, 1868-74, Liberal
Benjamin Disraeli, 1874-80, Conservative
William Ewart Gladstone, 1880-85, Liberal
Robert Gascoyne-Cecil, Marquess of Salisbury, 1885-86, Conservative
William Ewart Gladstone, 1886, Liberal
Robert Gascoyne-Cecil, Marquess of Salisbury, 1886-92, Conservative
William Ewart Gladstone, 1892-94, Liberal
The Earl of Rosebery, 1894-95, Liberal
Robert Gascoyne-Cecil, Marquess of Salisbury, 1895-1902, Conservative
Arthur James Balfour, 1902-05, Conservative
Henry Campbell-Bannerman, 1905-08, Liberal
Herbert Henry Asquith, 1908-16, Liberal
David Lloyd George, 1916-22, Liberal
Andrew Bonar Law, 1922-23, Conservative
Stanley Baldwin, 1923, Conservative
James Ramsay MacDonald, 1924, Labour
Stanley Baldwin, 1924-29, Conservative
James Ramsay MacDonald, 1929-35, Labour
Stanley Baldwin, 1935-37, Conservative
Arthur Neville Chamberlain, 1937-40, Conservative
Sir Winston Churchill, 1940-45, Conservative
Clement Richard Attlee, 1945-51, Labour
Sir Winston Churchill, 1951-55, Conservative
Anthony Eden, 1955-57, Conservative
Harold Macmillan, 1957-63, Conservative
Sir Alec Douglas-Home, 1963-64, Conservative
Harold Wilson, 1964-70, Labour
Edward Heath, 1970-74, Conservative
Harold Wilson, 1974-76, Labour
James Callaghan, 1976-79, Labour

Margaret Thatcher, 1979-90, Conservative
John Major, 1990-97, Conservative
Tony Blair, 1997-2007, Labour
Gordon Brown, 2007-10, Labour
David Cameron, 2010-present, Conservative

United States Presidents

George Washington, 1789-97, Independent
John Adams, 1797-1801, Federalist
Thomas Jefferson, 1801-09, Democratic-Republican
James Madison, 1809-17, Democratic-Republican
James Monroe, 1817-25, Democratic-Republican
John Quincy Adams, 1825-29, Democratic-Republican
Andrew Jackson, 1829-37, Democratic
Martin Van Buren, 1837-41, Democratic
William Henry Harrison, 1841, Whig
John Tyler, 1841-45, Whig, then no party
James K. Polk, 1845-49, Democratic
Zachary Taylor, 1849-50, Whig
Millard Fillmore, 1850-53, Whig
Franklin Pierce, 1853-57, Democratic
James Buchanan, 1857-61, Democratic
Abraham Lincoln, 1861-65, Republican
Andrew Johnson, 1865-69, Democratic
Ulysses S. Grant, 1869-77, Republican
Rutherford B. Hayes, 1877-81, Republican
James A. Garfield, 1881, Republican
Chester A. Arthur, 1881-85, Republican
Grover Cleveland, 1885-89, Democratic
Benjamin Harrison, 1889-93, Republican
Grover Cleveland, 1893-97, Democratic
William McKinley, 1897-1901, Republican
Theodore Roosevelt, 1901-09, Republican
William Howard Taft, 1909-13, Republican
Woodrow Wilson, 1913-21, Democratic
Warren G. Harding, 1921-23, Republican
Calvin Coolidge, 1923-29, Republican
Herbert Hoover, 1929-33, Republican
Franklin D. Roosevelt, 1933-45, Democratic

Harry S. Truman, 1945-53, Democratic
Dwight D. Eisenhower, 1953-61, Republican
John F. Kennedy, 1961-63, Democratic
Lyndon B. Johnson, 1963-69, Democratic
Richard Nixon, 1969-74, Republican
Gerald Ford, 1974-77, Republican
Jimmy Carter, 1977-81, Democratic
Ronald Reagan, 1981-89, Republican
George H.W. Bush, 1989-93, Republican
Bill Clinton, 1993-2001, Democratic
George W. Bush, 2001-09, Republican
Barack Obama, 2009-, Democratic

Prime Ministers of Australia, 1901 onwards

Edmund Barton, 1901-03
Alfred Deakin, Prime Minister three times: 1903-04, 1905-08 and 1909-10
Chris Watson, 1904
George Reid, 1904-05
Andrew Fisher, Prime Minister three times: 1908-09, 1910-13 and 1914-15
Joseph Cook, 1913-14
William Hughes, 1915-23
Stanley Bruce, 1923-29
James Scullin, 1929-32
Joseph Lyons, 1932-39
Earle Page, 1939
Robert Menzies, 1939-41 and 1949-66
Arthur Fadden, 1941
John Curtin, 1941-45
Francis Forde, 1945
Ben Chifley, 1945-49
Harold Holt, 1966-67
John McEwen, 1967-68
John Gorton, 1968-71
William McMahon, 1971-72
Gough Whitlam, 1972-75
Malcolm Fraser, 1975-83
Bob Hawke, 1983-91
Paul Keating, 1991-96
John Howard, 1996-2007

Kevin Rudd, 2007-10
Julia Gillard, 2010-13
Kevin Rudd, 2013-

Canadian Prime Ministers since Canadian Confederation in 1867

Sir John A. Macdonald, 1867-73
Alexander Mackenzie, 1873-78
Sir John A. Macdonald, 1878-91
Sir John Abbott, 1891-92
Sir John Thompson, 1892-94
Sir Mackenzie Bowell, 1894-96
Sir Charles Tupper, 1896
Sir Wilfrid Laurier, 1896-1911
Sir Robert Borden, 1911-20
Arthur Meighen, 1920-21
William Lyon Mackenzie King, 1921-26
Arthur Meighen, 1926
William Lyon Mackenzie King, 1926-30
Richard B Bennett, 1930-35
William Lyon Mackenzie King, 1935-48
Louis St Laurent, 1948-57
John Diefenbaker, 1957-63
Lester Pearson, 1963-68
Pierre Trudeau, 1968-79
Joe Clark, 1979-80
Pierre Trudeau, 1980-84
John Turner, 1984
Brian Mulroney, 1984-93
Kim Campbell, 1993
Jean Chrétien, 1993-2003
Paul Martin, 2003-06
Stephen Harper, 2006-

Bibliography

Books

Arnold, A.J., & McCartney, S., *George Hudson: The Rise and Fall of the Railway King*, Hambledon Continuum, London, 2004

Baker, W.J., *The History of the Marconi Company 1874-1965*, Routledge, London, 1970

Barry, Dr G. & Carruthers, L.A., *A History of Britain's Hospitals*, The Book Guild, Lewes, 2005

Black, A., *The First Ladies of the United States of America*, Scala, London, 2006

Canaday, M., *The Straight State: Sexuality and Citizenship in Twentieth-Century America*, Princeton University Press, 2009

Cassar, G.H., *Lloyd George at War, 1916-1918*, Anthem Press, London, 2010

Coulter, A., *Treason Liberal Treachery from the Cold War to the War on Terrorism*, Crown Forum, New York, 2003

Druckerman, P., *Lust in Translation: Infidelity from Tokyo to Tennessee*, Penguin, London, 2008

Gillen, M., *Assassination of the Prime Minister: The Shocking Death of Spencer Perceval*, Sidgwick & Jackson, London, 1972

Hanrahan, D., *The Assassination of the Prime Minister: John Bellingham and the Murder of Spencer Perceval*, Sutton Publishing, Stroud, 2008

Hyde, H.M., *Lord Reading: The Life of Rufus Isaacs, First Marquess of Reading*, Farrar, Straus and Giroux, New York, 1968

Jackson, S., *Rufus Isaacs, First Marquess of Reading*, Cassell, London, 1936

Kinsey, A., *Sexual Behaviour in the Human Male*, Indiana University Press, 1998

Latham, E., Varney, H. L. (ed.), *McCarthy as the Voice of People, The Meaning of McCarthyism*, D.C. Heath & Co., Massachusetts, 1973

Parris, M., & Maguire, K., *Great Parliamentary Scandals*, Robson Books, London, 1995

Reeves, T. (ed.), *McCarthyism*, Robert E. Krieger Publishing, Malabar, 1982

Rodriguez, V., *Women in Contemporary Mexican Politics*, University of Texas Press, 2003

Rogin, M., *The Intellectuals and McCarthy*, The M.I.T. Press, London/Massachusetts, 1967

Theoharis, A., *Seeds of Repression*, Quadrangle Books, New York, 1971

Thompson, J., *Political Scandal: Power and Visibility in the Media Age*, Polity, Cambridge, 2000

White, E., *The Beautiful Room is Empty*, Vintage, London, 1994

Williams, N. (ed.), *Arkansas Biography: A Collection of Notable Lives*, University of Arkansas Press, 2000

Zelizer, J., *Taxing America: Wilbur D. Mills, Congress and the State, 1945-1975*, Cambridge University Press, New York, 2000

Articles & Journals

'Taiwan Sex Video Star Hired as TV Anchor', *Bangkok Post*, 20 March 2007

'Top 10 Mistresses: Fanne Foxe', *Time* magazine, 1 July 2009

Goss, K.C., 'Congressman Wilbur D. Mills' Influence on Social Legislation', *Arkansas Historical Quarterly*, Vol. 54 (Spring 1995): Nos. 1-12

Hickman, M., 'Was Edwina Currie right about salmonella in eggs, after all?', *The Independent*, November 2006

Mayr, W., 'Corruption Scandals in Austria: A Web of Sleaze in Elegant Vienna', *Vienna Spiegel*, 13 October 2011

Rorabaugh, W.J., 'The Political Duel in the Early Republic: Burr v. Hamilton', *Journal of the Early Republic*, Vol. 15, No. 1, 1995

Wreszin, M., 'Media Manipulation, Partisan Politics, or Institutional Complicity', reviews in *American History*, Vol. 10, No. 2, 1982.

Websites

articleswhy.com

BBC news online

bigeye.com

biography.com/people/sally-hemings

bioguide.congress.gov

brainyquotes.com

harryhay.com

imdb.com

japantimes.co.jp

jewishvirtuallibrary.org

learnhistory.org.uk

lesbianlife.about.com

monticello.org

newworldencyclopedia.org

number10.gov.uk

nytimes.com

pbs.org

senate.gov

senatormccarthy.com

tjheritage.org

usnews.com

washingtonpost.com

womenshistory.about.org

Index

Discover **Your** His**tory**

Ancestors • Heritage • Memories

Each issue of *Discover Your History* presents special features and regular articles on a huge variety of topics about our social history and heritage – such as our ancestors, childhood memories, military history, British culinary traditions, transport history, our rural and industrial past, health, houses, fashions, pastimes and leisure ... and much more.

Historic pictures show how we and our ancestors have lived and the changing shape of our towns, villages and landscape in Britain and beyond.

Special tips and links help you discover more about researching family and local history. Spotlights on fascinating museums, history blogs and history societies also offer plenty of scope to become more involved.

Keep up to date with news and events that celebrate our history, and reviews of the latest books and media releases.

Discover Your History presents aspects of the past partly through the eyes and voices of those who were there.

Discover Your History is in all good newsagents and also available on subscription for six or twelve issues. For more details on how to take out a subscription and how to choose your free book, call 01778 392013 or visit **www.discoveryourhistory.net**